THE SYNERGETIC CLASSROOM

JOYFUL TEACHING AND GENTLE DISCIPLINE

C.M. Charles
San Diego State University

 LONGMAN

An imprint of Addison Wesley Longman, Inc.

New York • Reading, Massachusetts • Menlo Park, California • Harlow, England
Don Mills, Ontario • Sydney • Mexico City • Madrid • Amsterdam

Editor-in-Chief: Priscilla McGeehon
Acquisitions Editor: Virginia L. Blanford
Full Service Production Manager: Eric Jorgensen
Project Coordination, Text Design, and Page Makeup: Electronic Publishing Services Inc.,
N.Y.C.
Cover Designer/Manager: Nancy Danahy
Cover Illustration/Photo: © PhotoDisc, Inc.
Senior Print Buyer: Hugh Crawford
Printer and Binder: The Maple-Vail Book Manufacturing Group
Cover Printer: Coral Graphic Services

For permission to use copyrighted material, grateful acknowledgment is made to the copyright holders cited throughout this book which are hereby made part of this copyright page.

Library of Congress Cataloging-in-Publication Data

Charles, C.M.
      The synergetic classroom: joyful teaching and gentle discipline/
  C.M. Charles
        p. cm.
      Includes bibliographical references (p.) and index.
      ISBN 0-321-04912-8
      1. Classroom management.   2. School discipline.   I. Title.
LB3013.C4653 2000
371.102'4--dc21   99-34542
                                                               CIP

Please visit our website at http://www.awlonline.com

ISBN 0-321-04912-8

12345678910—MA—02010099

Chapter opener illustrations courtesy of C. M. Charles.

CONTENTS

CHAPTER 10

GENTLE DISCIPLINE IN THE SYNERGETIC CLASSROOM   *137*

CHAPTER 11

GETTING STARTED IN SYNERGETIC TEACHING AND DISCIPLINE   158

INTRODUCTION

The quality of public education in the United States and other countries of the West seems to be in slow but steady decline. Despite the vigorous efforts of educators, students now complete secondary school having learned less, on average, than they did decades ago. Universities regularly provide remedial courses to bring high school graduates up to standards formerly expected. Discipline problems at all levels of school have increased progressively, as has student apathy toward learning. Students still say they believe education is important but almost 50 percent of secondary students complain that school offers them little. They criticize lessons as boring and irrelevant to their lives. They say teachers are uninspiring and the curriculum out of touch with real life. Many of them say that, all in all, they get so little out of school they don't see any point in trying to learn.

Millions upon millions of dollars have been plowed into education in an attempt to reverse the decline. Teacher training has been overhauled. Magnet schools have been established in the performing arts, science and mathematics, physical education, and other specialties in hopes of motivating students. Early education programs have been put in place everywhere to give students a better start. Mentor teacher programs and in-service education intended to improve teaching have become standard in all school systems. But the results of these efforts have been disappointing. While pockets of true excellence shine here and there, the overall picture is dim.

As education worsens, fingers of blame are pointed in all directions. Choose your target: Societal values are in disarray. The family has broken down. Parents no longer support teachers and education. TV and home computers are more interesting than school. Violence rather than humane behavior is the major focus of the media. Drugs are making students mindless. Intimidating others has become the way to establish one's place in the world. Teacher training doesn't prepare teachers realistically. Tenure has removed teacher motivation to excel. Classes are too large. There are too many administrators. The curriculum is too watered down. The books students read, if they read at all, are insipid. There aren't enough computers in classrooms. Students' lives are too easy, too pampered. Students' lives are too difficult in this complex and demanding world. Too little money is spent on education. Too much money is spent on education. And so on.

All of these factors may be playing a part in dragging education down. Certainly some of them are. Teachers feel powerless. They don't see how they can do anything to correct a hedonistic society, the disintegrating family, the rampage of drugs, the appalling apathy of students, or the lack of support from parents. They can't make students behave or try to learn, but when students fail their classes and show disdain for education, teachers get the blame. It makes them want to throw in the towel.

Yet some teachers are notably successful. Their students learn, enjoy school, and appreciate education. Some of the graduates from public schools are among the most astute we have ever produced. What is going right for those teachers and students that is going wrong elsewhere? Do their schools have more money? Do they have better facilities? Do those teachers know something the rest of us don't?

Money and facilities don't have much to do with their good fortune, but yes, the teachers do seem to know something important about making teaching effective and learning enjoyable. They know they do the most good at the point where they interface personally with individual students. They know how to rally students to them. They know how to build trust. They know how to strengthen student dignity and capitalize on it, rather than inadvertently saying or doing things that damage relations. They know how to communicate. They know how to help students resolve conflicts and maintain positive feelings. They know how to make lessons consistently interesting. They know how to use their personal charisma. By doing these things, they energize students, help them find enjoyment in school, and teach them skills and information of value. Students in turn respect those teachers, involve themselves in learning, and behave responsibly. In these classes, discipline problems are few and far between. Learning is busy and satisfying. Camaraderie is evident. Students and teacher feed energy to each other, producing the exhilaration in learning that most people experience only rarely.

That kind of teaching, herein called **synergetic teaching**, can extricate education from the quagmire in which it is bogged. More money is not the answer, nor are fancier schools or glitzier equipment. Supportive parents would be nice, but we can manage in their absence. Less media enthrallment with the worst in society would be helpful, but we can supply humaneness to offset it. It would be easier if we had students whose psyches were less damaged, but we can work with their strengths. It is a rare student, regardless of background, who cannot or will not respond to teachers who are trustworthy, kind, caring, and helpful, and who take a personal interest in them and make learning fun rather than dull.

Most of us can retool ourselves to teach in this way. But first we must recognize that our curriculum, activities, and discipline too often run contrary to students' needs and natures. We expect students, even when bored silly, to pay attention, show interest, and do as told. When they don't, we try to force them, seemingly not realizing that force produces emotions that shut off learning. We defeat ourselves by always telling students what to do while not allowing them to make decisions about their life in school. We miss the mark worst of all when we damage their dignity and trust.

This book is intended to help all teachers work in the ways that have brought success to a fortunate few. It reveals no deep secrets but does point out serious errors commonly made in teaching and tells how to remedy them. It explains how to work intentionally *with* students rather than inadvertently *against* them. It tells how to reduce student resistance by providing interesting activities and allowing students to learn in ways they enjoy. It tells how to communicate effectively, solve problems, and resolve conflicts. It tells how to earn students' trust so they will want to follow your lead. And finally, it shows how to reduce discipline problems to a minimum and deal easily with the few that occur.

Teachers have two great dreams—to work with students who try to learn, and to escape from the constant struggle against misbehavior. Synergetic teaching and discipline can help deliver those dreams. It can cause your students to learn, behave themselves, and give you respect. They will behave themselves because they want to. You will enjoy them, and they you. You can accomplish this by putting in place nine elements of teaching that lead to synergy—that exhilarating state where everyone is involved and creativity abounds. Synergetic teaching and discipline remove most causes of misbehavior. When occasional misbehavior occurs, gentle intervention brings satisfactory resolution and leaves feelings intact.

With synergetic teaching and discipline in place, you can look forward to each day and go home at night pleasantly tired rather than raggedly frustrated. You may not attain these results all the time, but this much can be promised: If you conscientiously apply what is advocated in this book, your relations with students will improve markedly. Students will become more cooperative. Their misbehavior will decline, and you will have to expend only a fraction of your former effort on discipline. Teaching will become what you always hoped it might be.

1
DISCIPLINE, TEACHING, AND THE MYSTERIOUS SYNERGETIC RELATIONSHIP

Mr. Higganbotham, I forget... is having us memorize
Lincoln's Gettysburg Address working with or against
our adolescent nature?

In the pages that follow, you'll find a new perspective on classroom teaching and discipline. Although we begin by focusing on discipline, because teachers for decades have identified classroom discipline as the toughest problem they face, we will soon move attention to teaching. As we proceed, you will see that the distinctions between the two blur because in teaching done at its best, instruction and discipline are not separate entities. They are part of the same process. Of course, most teachers do not think of them that way.

When teachers use the word **discipline**, they mean either of two things: One is the relative degree to which **misbehavior is evident** in the classroom. When they see a classroom where students are disrupting, goofing off, refusing to work, annoying others, cheating, or defying the teacher, they will say, "The discipline in that class is terrible!" The other meaning refers to what teachers **do to control** misbehavior.

Within that meaning you hear teachers say, "Bob Johns has a great system of discipline." Or, "Bob Johns can really discipline students." You can see from these examples that discipline is thought of something we **do to students** to make them behave. However, that view has little validity in high quality teaching, as we shall see.

THE PROBLEM OF DISCIPLINE

Misbehavior is the most difficult problem teachers have to contend with. It is a problem because it interferes with teaching and learning, shortchanges students, and comes close to driving teachers nuts. You might think that after decades of grappling with their worst problem, teachers would have devised a way to ensure proper behavior. Indeed, every teacher has a bag of tricks accumulated from experience and lore, and in addition has access to a number of highly touted commercial programs. If you are a teacher or about to become one, you've heard of some of them: Assertive Discipline, Cooperative Discipline, Positive Discipline, Positive Discipline in the Classroom, Discipline with Dignity, Discipline from within. All are well organized and have their good points. The trouble is that they don't seem to be making permanent improvements in student behavior.

It is as if misbehavior becomes resistant to every new remedy that appears. Teachers begin to feel overwhelmed. They see misbehavior growing worse and have begun to believe they can't do anything about it. They blame fragmented families, bad genes, slum neighborhoods, drugs, abandonment of personal responsibility, loss of respect for authority, hedonism, and a society that increasingly just doesn't care. All of those conditions take their toll, and if they were the real causes of poor behavior, teachers would be lost. Teachers can't strengthen families, eliminate hedonism, improve living conditions, or eradicate drugs, nor can they do anything to improve the genes responsible for human nature. There are many things about society and humans we'd all like to change, but we can't. In any case, when it comes to classroom discipline, society and genetics and all the other factors being blamed are essentially immaterial. The fact is that they are not the root causes of misbehavior. When we lay blame on them, we only strike the nail a glancing blow. We do not hit it on the head.

THE REAL CAUSE OF THE PROBLEM

Students do not misbehave randomly. They do so for particular reasons, which are neither mysterious nor psychologically impenetrable. The reasons are rather evident and all of them can be eliminated, modified, or avoided by teachers in the classroom. Here are the reasons why students misbehave:

1. Some students like to *probe at existing boundaries* to see how far they can push and what they can get away with. When they go too far, we say they are misbehaving.
2. Students *mimic each other*, especially when disapproved behavior is involved.
3. From time to time, students will be *intensely curious about or interested in* something, so strongly that they disregard teacher directions.
4. Most students *crave attention* and if necessary will misbehave to get it.
5. Most students *want power*, especially in matters that affect themselves. They often defy the teacher to prove they have power.
6. When students become *bored or frustrated*, they will disengage from assigned tasks and look for more interesting things to do, often things that are disapproved.
7. At times a student will be in a *bad mood*, perhaps from something that happened outside the class, and will withdraw or treat others inconsiderately.
8. When students' *dignity* (sense of self as a respected person) *is threatened*, they often lash back with verbal or physical aggression.
9. Occasionally students will become embroiled in disagreements that escalate and *boil over disruptively* in the class.
10. A few students have such egocentric personalities they think *anything they do is all right*, including intimidation and malicious retaliation when they don't get their way.

Most teachers struggle continually with misbehavior. Their primary aim is to suppress it. But that never solves the problem. Rather than fighting against misbehavior teachers need to identify the cause and correct it. Causes of misbehavior are tied in closely with human nature. Wise teachers avoid working at cross-purposes with students' needs and feelings. Teaching and discipline reach their highest quality when they are in concert with student nature. That requires adapting teaching to student needs and traits or, if that is not appropriate (as it would not be with students who have overblown egos), it means working around idiosyncrasies that contribute to misbehavior. In school we often forbid students to behave as their makeup urges them to do. At the same time we try to force them to do what their natures tell them to avoid. We bring trouble down on our own heads by persisting in this self-defeating mismatch.

Think about human nature. All of us, including the young, want to talk, laugh, and have pleasant relations with our friends. These behaviors are not always appropriate in the classroom, but when they are they should be allowed during learning. All of us, including the young, do some unattractive things, such as lying and talking back derogatorily, usually to protect our sense of self, our personal dignity. We do not behave in this way except when our dignity is threatened or when we fear we'll be punished. All of us, including the young, hate boredom. We despise it so much we can never for long resist looking for something interesting to do. Unfortunately, what interests Sammy can throw Ms. Bledsoe into panic. All of us, including the young, resist being made to do anything. When forced, we dig in our heels. We would probably pitch a fuss even if somebody made us eat ice cream every day.

We cannot do much to change these natural behaviors in ourselves and the young. (You may have noted that they are called "misbehavior" only when an adult identifies them as disruptive, defiant, or immoral.) In normal discipline, teachers try to keep a lid on them. But natural behavior is like popcorn. When the kernels begin to explode, you just can't keep the pan's lid from blowing off.

THE SOLUTION TO THE PROBLEM

If we can't change students' natural inclinations, and if those inclinations produce behavior that is destructive to teaching and learning, what can we do? There are only two viable options, it would seem. One is to continue discipline as it is practiced today. This approach suppresses undesired behavior, keeps it under wraps, below the surface, under control—up to a point. Formerly we did this harshly, with stern talk, threat, intimidation, and punishment. Nowadays we call that **old-fashioned discipline**. More recently we have tried using softer approaches. We have cut down on intimidation. We talk more with students, let them help make rules of behavior for the class, and decide on mild punishment to be used when rules are broken. We give out rewards when students behave as we desire. We sometimes call this approach **modern discipline**. It is the approach taken in most of today's popular systems of discipline.

The softness in modern discipline is evident in the gentle words teachers use and in their humane concern for their students. But at heart modern discipline still tries to **force** students to behave in certain ways. That's why we are so often disappointed. Students balk when forced. So modern discipline, even though the harshness has been removed, still works against human nature. It is only a matter of time until it breaks down. Instead of enlivening students and motivating them to work, modern discipline mostly tells them what *not* to do. Coercion—making students do this and forbidding them to do that— is the fatal flaw in modern discipline.

The second option available to teachers is to **work with, rather than against, student nature**. Since students want to talk and laugh, why not give them learning activities that allow them to do so? If they hate boredom, why not make lessons interesting? If they are apathetic, why not energize the class? If they require reaffirmation of personal identity and belonging, why not provide what they need? If they want to feel personally appreciated, why not show them they are? If they are determined to preserve personal dignity, why not help them do so? By working with student nature rather than against it you automatically reduce misbehavior dramatically. Moreover, you almost never have to pit your will against that of your students. And no, they won't run wild. To the contrary, they have little reason to misbehave when their needs are being met. If they get off-track, you counsel and guide, but you have no need for force. When things are going very well you can forget about discipline, at least as something you tack onto teaching. This will make you will feel immensely better about your students, their accomplishments, and yourself. Guaranteed.

The goals of this book are to help make teaching joyful and discipline easy. These goals are accomplished by working *with* student nature rather than against it. The approach is aimed at developing **synergy** in the class, hence the labels *synergetic teaching* and *synergetic discipline*. Synergy is a state characterized by high energy, creativity, and production. The people or other entities involved in synergy feed psychic energy to each other. When this happens in the classroom, it gives teachers and students those peak educational experiences that leave them exhilarated. Synergy sometimes occurs spontaneously, but teachers don't know how to call it forth on demand. This book shows you how to do so. You can bring it to life, control it, and use it to your advantage. When you teach synergetically, students begin to work together willingly and harmoniously, not because they are made to but because they want to. It is fun and exciting. No discipline is required. This frees you to give better guidance and assistance. Students do higher quality work and are proud of it and themselves. And you? Long accustomed to frustration, you are now glowing with satisfaction.

Utopian? It sounds so, but this is not pie in the sky. It is all attainable. As will be shown later, you can cause it to happen by building trust with students, intriguing them, enticing them to cooperate, and involving them in activities that meet their needs. You don't ever have to *make them* do anything at all. You can actually do what teachers have always been told *not* to do—be friends with your students. You listen to their concerns, attend to their needs, and provide assistance. You help them meet their goals and they, in turn, help you meet yours.

As for synergetic discipline, you will find no need for a set of tactics to impose when students misbehave. You will have no need for punishment. No negative consequences. No detention slips. No sending students to study rooms for time-outs. No public embarrassment. No hassle on your part, no anger, no frustration. You begin building toward the synergetic state the first day of class. You put in place certain elements, identified later in this chapter. As those elements interact, they produce a surprising effect—they energize and motivate students and influence them to work harmoniously. Suddenly there are no "sides"—no student side of issues and no teacher side. Both of you work together toward the same end. Imagine working with students instead of against them—that is every teacher's dream.

DOROTHY VALE, ONE WHO DIDN'T HAVE IT (MEANING DISCIPLINE)

Many years ago I had the demoralizing experience of supervising Dorothy Vale as she struggled in student teaching. The struggle didn't last long. Within weeks it was clear Dorothy would fail. All of us—master teacher, principal, and myself—did our best to help her, but we were incapable of it. After all these years I still feel bad about the anguish she went through and my inability to rescue her. Dorothy seemed so well suited to teaching. She had raised three children into their teenage years. She had worked part-time in a pre-school and her husband was a high school history teacher. She was intelligent and tried hard. The problem was that she couldn't control second-grade students, little tots seven and eight years old. Can you believe it? (Many second-grade teachers can.) She tried commanding, pleading, scolding, warning, and sweet-talking, but she might as well have been mumbling in her sleep. She never had a chance, really. The children ran all over her, sometimes literally. After four weeks of ceaseless frustration, she was in despair. Anybody who talked with her about it encountered a deluge of tears.

All of us gave Dorothy our best effort. Mrs. Dosser, the master teacher in whose classroom Dorothy was placed, talked with her endlessly and repeatedly demonstrated what to do and say when giving directions, presenting the lesson, and assisting students at their seats. The techniques that were effective for Mrs. Dosser didn't work for Dorothy. I made a number of erudite professorial suggestions that were all colossal flops. Finally Mr. Bradley, the principal, intervened, which normally he never did. He reprimanded the children and lectured them on manners. They sat quietly after that for a while, but once he was gone and Dorothy was back in charge they made up for lost time.

At the middle of the semester, the decision about Dorothy was made. Mr. Bradley, Mrs. Dosser, and I sat in Mr. Bradley's office. School was out for the day and the grounds were quiet. I can still see the impulse sprinkler rhythmically sending a great sweep of water back and forth across the lawn, symbolically sweeping Dorothy away.

"I think we better take her out," I said. "I could probably place her somewhere else, but from what I've seen I don't think she can make it in teaching."

Mrs. Dosser was feeling guilty, thinking she had let Dorothy down. "I've been trying my best to show her," she said quietly. "Maybe if she stays with me a little longer . . . Maybe we could start again and work her into it more slowly."

Mr. Bradley, a fine gentleman who had once been a fighter pilot and was now nearing retirement, said, "I don't know. We can't let those kids run wild anymore. It's bad for them. We have to think of them first, not Dorothy, bless her heart."

We dawdled, not saying much or drinking our coffee. It was a sad time. Mr. Bradley said, "You know, over the years I have learned something about teachers. When it comes to discipline, to controlling kids, you've either got it or you don't. There's not much in between. It is hard to say just what the 'it' is. Something in their personality. But you can usually tell right away whether a person has it or not. If they do, they will be successful in teaching. If they don't, they will have nothing but trouble. Dorothy just doesn't have it."

A few decades have gone by since that day. Mr. Bradley has passed away, but I often think of his words: You either have it or you don't. Even Mr. Bradley couldn't say what "it" was, but he could tell if a teacher had it or not. So could I. Anyhow, Dorothy didn't have it. She completed her degree but gave up on teaching. She was happy with that decision, she told me later. She found a pleasant niche working in a teacher supply store. She didn't want to say much about her student teaching. I came forth with a fine platitude about how things have a way of working out. It was true in her case.

GRADATIONS OF THE IT

The way Mr. Bradley saw things, to "have it" was to be able to control the class. Never mind how control was achieved. It could be through sweetness, persuasion, intimidation, threat . . . the technique didn't matter. Teachers who could control the class were successful because they got their lessons taught. Students learned the material and behaved in a civil manner. Teachers who could not control their classes were unsuccessful. Their students didn't pay attention, were boisterous, and didn't learn much.

Mr. Bradley knew that among the teachers who had it, some were loved by their students while others were feared or hated. He knew that some classrooms hummed with purposeful activity and good spirit while others were like cold detention centers. The difference didn't worry him much. For Mr. Bradley the bottom lines were learning and good behavior. If a teacher got those, especially good behavior, that was what mattered.

This is not to suggest that Mr. Bradley was out of touch. His view was prevalent through the 1960s and is still much with us today. He was a dedicated school man, very concerned that students learned and behaved civilly. Students were a bit afraid of him, but he was loved by his teachers. He was a kind gentleman who brooked little nonsense and stood firmly for what he believed. Many of his teachers, perhaps most, shared his views.

Yet we now know that his concept of "having it or not" is greatly misleading. It is true that most people when entering teaching fall into one of two groups—those who can naturally maintain order in the classroom and those who cannot. It is also true that those who never become able to control the class either fail or lead intensely frustrating lives. It is good when such people leave teaching, for their students' sake and their own. But among the "have it" group are many who can damage students as much as the "have not" group. We've all experienced those teachers, those who rule through threat and fear. They are found at all levels, from kindergarten through graduate school. They are no longer allowed to inflict physical pain, but they willingly use psychological tactics that cause lasting hurt.

MR. MASON AND THE FEARSOME IT

Aubry Mason taught eight-grade general math. He would have been much appreciated by Mr. Bradley. When I first knew him, his students learned and there was no misbehavior in his classes. None. That was not because he filled students with love of learning. They behaved themselves because they were scared to death of him. As a lesson presenter, Mr. Mason was skillful, efficient, and clear. That didn't carry much weight with students. Most of them dreaded his classes. They put more study into math than any other subject, but only because they lived in terror of being called on the next day. They knew if Mr. Mason asked them a question, their responses, unless perfect, would bring on the dreaded Mason stare where Mr. Mason locked onto their eyes and held . . . and held . . . and held, until he made sweat ooze from every pore. Mr. Mason didn't believe in moving on to someone else when a kid's response fell short of perfection. He never smiled nor offered a helpful hint or word of encouragement. The only thing he gave freely was sarcastic remarks about the students' effort and character.

Yet most people considered Mr. Mason a good teacher. That included at least a few of his students, once they were removed from his glare. But no student would ever have gone to his class willingly or voluntarily approached him or said to a friend, "There is a teacher I admire." Mr. Mason, unlike Dorothy Vale, had it. But the "it" he had was one of force and intimidation. If Mr. Mason had only made learning more adventuresome, he need never have relied on intimidation. Apparently he didn't know that.

Mr. Mason retired in 1988. He was glad to get out of teaching. Things had changed for him. He didn't look back on his career with satisfaction.

He had nothing good to say about the day's students—those impolite, inconsiderate, unmotivated slobs, as he called some of them. They seemed that way to him because he could no longer make them toe the line. His control techniques had lost their effectiveness. Students no longer sweated and stammered under his glare. They weren't so afraid of him anymore, and if called on they might just shrug their shoulders and say, "I don't know." If he said, "For your paltry efforts, you earn a grade of F," they might well reply, "Okay by me," and mutter, "Who gives a (bleep)?" Mr. Mason, by the time his career ended, realized that he was no longer a successful teacher. He blamed that not on himself, but on the students. Not all students were at fault, of course. But enough were. Though Mr. Mason never seemed aware of it, even those who knuckled under harbored resentment toward him and the subjects he taught. I have no doubt that over his career Mr. Mason caused hundreds of students to develop a permanent aversion to mathematics.

Violet Cooper and the Good It

Proper class behavior is as necessary today as it ever was. We can no longer obtain it with the old-fashioned ways. But because fortune sometimes smiles, we can have something even better. We can entice students to cooperate and make a genuine effort to learn. We can establish a humane environment conducive to learning—a place where students are treated with kindness and respect and where they, in turn, treat us and each other the same. We can make the classroom a place of stimulation, interest, and purposeful activity. Within that environment, we can relate comfortably with students, draw (not force) them into learning, and become their mentors, champions, and trusted allies. Not many of us accomplish this, however.

Violet Cooper, a contemporary of Mr. Mason, was one who did. Unlike Dorothy, Violet had it. Unlike Mr. Mason, her "it" was positive, not negative; welcoming, not daunting. Until she retired, Violet taught middle school science. Everybody called her a natural. She almost never had a discipline problem, but when she did she handled it quickly and quietly. She didn't get upset and didn't make the transgressing kid sweat, seethe, or dream of blowing up her car. She was as skillful as Mr. Mason at presenting lessons, but provided kids a great bonus— she made her lessons interesting. Her students learned and behaved themselves. She never scolded, threatened, or used sarcasm. On occasions she did tell the class she felt uneasy about what she saw or heard in the room, or disappointed about the progress that was being made, and asked the students if they could help her understand why. She enjoyed having students stay and chat after school. Former students frequently dropped by to say hello. Even parents sought her out to express their appreciation.

I placed several student teachers with Violet. All were in awe of her and tried to emulate her style. A couple of times I invited Violet to attend student-teaching seminars. Student teachers were always in turmoil over discipline, and I thought there would be nobody better than Violet to tell them how to keep good control. Find out from the best, that's how I figured it. But Violet's presentations in the seminars were disappointing. She admitted up front that she couldn't put her finger on any particular thing she said or did that caused students to behave well. She told anecdotes and passed along platitudes, such as have faith in the kids, trust them, always treat them with respect, don't get upset when they do childish things, and always allow them a second, third, or fourth chance. I was thinking uh-oh. Imagine giving that advice to Dorothy Vale. And to Mr. Mason? Forget it. As Violet said those things, my student teachers nodded in agreement. They liked the sound-good credibility of Violet's philosophy. But once Violet was gone, they became restive. I had lauded Violet too much. They expected her not only to say lovely things about trusting students, but to provide a short list of easily applied techniques guaranteed to convert incipient devils into instant angels. (To be truthful, I thought she would, too, and was as disappointed as my students.) At that time we couldn't put Violet's thoughts into a recipe—we couldn't identify any steps to take. Well, neither could she. Not much help there.

THE MUTUALLY-ENHANCING PHENOMENON

Now we can pretty much make sense of what Violet was getting at. We have learned that the best discipline comes not from a set of steps, but from how we interact with students on a daily basis. We can also identify what Violet did that placed her above Dorothy and Mr. Mason. It is embarrassing that it took so long to figure out. What Violet did was this: She established **mutually enhancing relationships** with her students. She didn't realize she was doing that. She thought she was just showing them kindness and respect and they were doing the same back to her. She didn't consider there was anything artful about it: It was just the right thing to do. She realized that students prized their own dignity more than most everything else. She helped them maintain it and in her lessons provided considerable interest and support. Motivation and energy grew as a result and productive learning followed. She didn't do this to raise her energy level and job satisfaction. It may sound stupid to say, but she did it because she loved her students. She often said she did and no doubt meant it, not in a sappy or altruistic sense, but as we love friends who share our burdens and bring joy to our lives.

THE SYNERGETIC RELATIONSHIP

The mutually enhancing relationship, like that which Violet achieved so well with her students, is what in this book we call a **synergetic relationship**.

Later we will explore specifics of synergetic teaching and discipline and see how they are initiated and used. Synergetic is an adjective related to the noun synergy. Synergy can occur physically or psychologically. In physical synergy, two or more objects, chemicals, or body organs function together to produce an overall effect that is greater, often much greater, than the sum of the individual effects.

We can illustrate this concept by using an analogous phenomenon. If you have ever been around campfires, you may have seen two smoldering logs lying in the fire ring, both glowing and giving off heat but neither producing flames. If you push the logs close together each transfers energy into the other. If there is sufficient mutual energy, they will eventually burst into flame, giving off vastly more heat and light than the two were giving off individually. Of course, there is not always enough energy to make them flame. Placing two cold logs side by side leaves both as cold as before. Sometimes, the necessary ingredients for synergy are present; sometimes they are not.

In teaching, we are concerned with psychological synergy. You have experienced it many times in social situations and perhaps in school or at work. It occurs when your thoughts and behaviors interact in a certain way with those of others. It can produce a variety of emotions including joy and excitement. With these emotions, energy and motivation usually increase. The most prized effect for teachers is student motivation. When the interaction is positive, students become eager to involve themselves in productive tasks. This in and of itself substantially reduces misbehavior. Students' ideas are more abundant and creative and their work is of higher quality. Their energy is not consumed, leaving them worn out and needing change. High levels of vitality remain even after tasks are completed.

But just as physical synergy does not occur under all circumstances, neither does psychological synergy. Bringing two or more students together may not do a single thing for any of them. Certain enabling elements must be present before synergy can occur. Presently we will review those elements and in later chapters will see how they are put in place.

WHY THE TITLE "SYNERGETIC TEACHING AND DISCIPLINE?"

As said earlier, the beginning focus of this book is on classroom discipline, on dealing with the dreaded *bête noire* of teaching. Before 1960, not much was known or written about classroom discipline. Those of us who entered teaching in that era were unofficially advised to present a serious front and to use stern speech and a heavy hand to enforce proper behavior. I was actually told not to smile at first nor be too friendly. I was to be business-like, professional, serious—that's what my mentors said. Once I had my students behaving properly, I could loosen up a bit, though with caution. I understood that being too lax in the beginning was to invite certain disaster, meaning an uncontrollable class.

Since that time, useful and respected discipline systems have been introduced. They have instructed teachers on how to establish rules, provide reasonable consequences when rules are broken, reward proper student behavior, communicate effectively, teach in a democratic manner, and involve students in making decisions. As mentioned earlier, most of these programs are designed to make students behave properly. They remain mildly coercive and still depict discipline as something separate and apart from teaching, an add-on set of tactics to make students be quiet, orderly, hard working, and respectful.

In the best classes, like those of Violet Cooper, it is virtually impossible to distinguish between teaching and discipline. If you examine the synergy in her class and try to separate discipline from teaching, you come to realize that the two are basically the same, as are the processes that bring them about. The student who normally works lethargically, if at all, works willingly when energized and motivated. The student continually at odds with the teacher or fellow students becomes cooperative when trust is established. The student who talks out disruptively (far and away the main "misbehavior" in classrooms) learns, through a supportive relationship with the teacher, whether talking, and how much of it, is appropriate in various learning activities. Discipline is not something different from teaching. It is an integral part of it.

But even though synergetic teaching and discipline may be identical at the core, now is not a propitious time to drop the term discipline. Teachers are wary of a back alley into which they have been lured before—one called "if you are a good enough teacher you won't have discipline problems." Not many teachers will go for that again. Still, the basic notion is credible if you remove the "good enough teacher" and say instead that "a certain kind of teaching can vastly reduce misbehavior and make it easier to deal with what does occur." That is a reality we can expect in synergetic teaching and discipline. In years to come, discipline, which for so long has plagued teachers, will likely disappear into the folds of good teaching.

The Promise of Synergetic Teaching and Discipline

How would you, as a teacher, like to work with students who are motivated to learn, considerate of others, respectful toward you, appreciative of what you do for them, willing to work hard, and resourceful and creative? "Gee, I think it might be all right," you say. "And while you are at it, I'd also like a salary of $1 million a year, plus benefits."

You can have it. It is there for the taking. (All except the $1 million plus benefits.) Maybe not to perfection, but to a degree greater than you would think. Admittedly, teaching will never be completely without concerns and problems. But most teachers would take a daily swim in ice water for a guaranteed 50 percent improvement over what they now experience. That amount of improvement and more is within immediate reach. You only have to put synergetic teaching and discipline in place. The synergetic approach will energize rather than debilitate, reward rather than frustrate. It will make teaching better for you and learning better for your students. No more balkiness and lethargy from them (or you). That will be gone in favor of eagerness and cooperation. That is the natural result when we work *with* someone rather than against them.

To accomplish synergy, you must establish trust with your students. You have to take the first steps, but students will become trusting of you in return when they see you are completely for them. You can guide and support them as they seek to make what they can of their lives. You can help them learn things they genuinely need or that strongly interest them. You can organize instruction so it meets, rather than thwarts, their needs for belonging, hope, fun, freedom, competence, and power. You can communicate with them in ways that confer dignity and encourage responsibility, without doing anything contrary to their best interest.

THE NINE ELEMENTS NEEDED FOR SYNERGY

Nine elements, used in conjunction, permit synergetic teaching and discipline to occur fully. The path you will follow through this book takes you to each of these elements and shows you how to incorporate it into teaching. The following are the elements needed for synergetic teaching and discipline:

1. **Ethics**. This element is fundamental and is your sole responsibility. You must dedicate yourself to being an ethical teacher. To help with this, you will explore the ethics required when working with students, what it means for a teacher to function ethically, and why ethics provide the only foundation upon which synergetic teaching and discipline can stand.
2. **Trust**. You will see that it is necessary for you to establish trust with every one of your students. You will see how trust comes from ethics and will explore the dynamics by which trusting relationships are developed, sustained, and lost.
3. **Charisma.** You will examine what it means to have charisma and why students eagerly follow charismatic teachers. You will see that charisma comes not just from an outgoing personality, but also from unusual experiences, artistic or other special talents, story telling ability, imagination, special interests and hobbies, family life, and the like.
4. **Communication**. The process by which synergy is achieved depends greatly on the nature of class communication and how it is initiated and sustained. You will learn what kind of communication serves best, the conditions that encourage it, how communication can help and harm relationships, and specific communication skills that lead to synergy.

5. **Interest**. The learning activities to which you invite students must be made interesting enough to attract and hold their involvement. You will learn how to organize activities so they intrigue students and satisfy their needs.

6. **Class agreements**. You will need to reach agreements with your students concerning life in the classroom—how the class will function, how you will teach and relate to students, how students will behave toward each other, how they will discharge their responsibilities, and how the group will resolve problems that might occur. Thoughtful student input is essential. You will need to monitor and appraise these agreements to evaluate their effectiveness, always with an eye to making improvements.

7. **Coopetition**. Coopetition is a label coined by combining the words cooperation and competition. It combines the best qualities of each while eliminating the poorer qualities. It means "cooperating to compete." You will explore the natures of cooperation and competition and examine their advantages and disadvantages. You will then learn how to use coopetition to energize students and bring out the best in them.

8. **Human relations**. During every class period many opportunities occur for you to teach human relations skills to your students. These skills help develop trust and enable people to work together more effectively. They also help us build ourselves as we admire and show respect for others.

9. **Problem resolution**. Problems come with teaching. To a large degree your happiness and success depend on how well you can resolve problems and conflicts, both those that involve misbehavior and those that do not. You will see how class problems can be resolved productively and conflicts settled to everyone's satisfaction, while preserving dignity and maintaining trust.

These, then, are the nine elements that, when used in conjunction with each other, can bring us the benefits of synergy. None of the elements is outside your reach. Putting them in place requires a bit of learning and a change in the way you work with your students. The elements can be put in place fairly easily. The remainder of this book explains how that is done.

Figure 1.1 shows the nine elements that combine to produce synergy. Trust is placed in the center because it always affects class interactions. Developing trust is your responsibility. Beginning at the top of the figure and moving clockwise you see the elements of ethics, charisma, communication and interest. These elements are almost solely your responsibility too. Continuing on, you see the elements of class agreements, coopetition, human relations, and problem resolution. You and the students share responsibility for those elements.

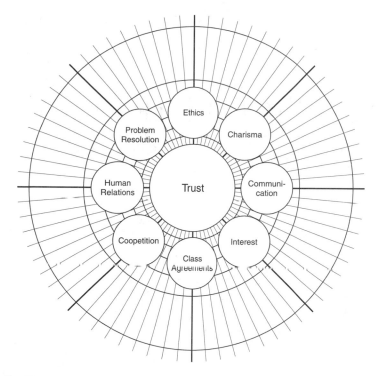

Figure 1.1 The synergy sunburst.

To Think About

1. Can you recall a teacher you had who was poor in discipline?
   Did you like that teacher as a person? What seemed to be the
   reason he or she could not maintain class control?
2. Think back on the two or three best teachers you ever had.
   What did they do or have that causes you to identify them as
   exceptional teachers?
3. Think of occasions when you have experienced synergy. What
   were the occasions? Who was involved? What level of trust—
   high, moderate, or low—did you have with those involved?
4. Review the elements needed for synergy. Do you think synergy ever occurs in the absence of some of the elements? Which
   three do you consider to be most essential for excellent teaching and discipline? Which three do you consider least essential? Are there some that could be left out altogether without
   decreasing synergy over time? Explain your conclusions.

2

YOUR ETHICAL SELF: HOW YOUR VIRTUE LEADS TO TRUST

Mrs. Luna, Carl here wanted me to ask if you've made any deposits in our trust accounts lately?

THE DISTRESSING MR. WOAK:

When I was a student in seventh grade, I had an incident with a teacher, Mr. Woak, that left me distrustful of him and forever resentful of the way he treated me. To this day I consider him the epitome of what a teacher should not be. My family had just moved from a city to a small farming community, and I arrived at my new school in the middle of a semester. The class was woodworking shop. All the workstations in the shop had been assigned to other students. Mr. Woak told me that if a student was absent I should use the vacant work area for the day, and if there were no vacant places, to find another student who would let me share a space. He then left me to fend for myself. The assignment being worked on at the time was to make a dado cut in a slat of wood, using a saw and chisel, so that another piece of wood could be fitted into the slot. This was a first step in making a magazine rack. Mr. Woak showed us how to do the task and told us that if we got it right on the first or second try, we would get a grade of A. I found a vacant place, got my materials and tools, and went dutifully, if timidly, to work. I carefully measured and marked the lines, sawed them, and chiseled out the middle. I took my work to Mr. Woak. He checked it with the test block. It didn't quite fit. Mr. Woak told me to do it again. The next day, there were no vacant places. I selected the smallest, frailest kid and asked if I could share his space. He nodded and I went to work on the cut again. While we were working, Mr. Woak walked around the shop with a slat of wood in his hand. He liked to pop students on the butt with it, in a friendly way if they were doing good, but with more force if they were goofing off. I was lost in work when I heard a splat and felt fire in my posterior. I wheeled around. Mr. Woak's hawk-like face was glaring at me. "Get back to your own place," he commanded, apparently having forgotten the instructions he gave me the previous day. "I ain't got no own place," I replied. I don't know how I came up with that particular grammatical construction, as no one in my family spoke that way. Probably that was how I thought country kids talked. Mr. Woak frowned, thought, and then said, "Oh, yes. Well, get back to work." At the end of the period I reluctantly showed Mr. Woak my completed work. He tested it and said, "Yes, well, I suppose that's all right." Mr. Woak put our grades up on a chart at the end of each assignment. The next day I checked the chart and found, beside my name, a grade of B. Clearly, the letter had originally been a printed capital A. It had been written over two or three times and made into a B, though I had done the assignment properly on the second try. I was too afraid of Mr. Woak to say anything about it, and though I liked working with wood, I thereafter dreaded going to the class. Mercifully, it ended two months, one magazine rack, and one lamp stand later.

I wasn't alone in my abhorrence of Mr. Woak. I heard other thirteen-year-old boys vow they would catch him out somewhere and "whip his ass." That was a favorite expression of early adolescent machismo in that particular place and time, though of course no boy would actually try such a thing, or at least wouldn't in those days. Anyhow, I'd be very surprised if Mr. Woak ever experienced the faintest glimmer of synergy in his classes. I doubt if he ever got anything out of teaching except a paycheck and an opportunity to wield power over kids. That was probably enough to satisfy him, the old grouch.

What did I expect of Mr. Woak? Not perfection, surely, but I expected him to be a decent man. More accurately, I expected him to be a decent person *as a teacher*. I would never know if he kicked his dog or sassed his wife. But in the classroom, even way back then, we wanted teachers to be truthful, helpful, and kind. We wanted our teachers to be ethical. That's what students of all ages still want.

WHY ETHICS ARE IMPORTANT

Are you an ethical teacher? Or if you are not yet teaching do you believe you will in the future be judged ethical? You are not being interrogated here, but you really must answer that question fairly. It's important because you must be ethical in everything students see you do and hear you say. If you are, they will come to trust you. The young, provided they have been adequately nurtured, are naturally inclined to trust adults. But if an adult treats them unethically—that is, badly—they withdraw their trust. You can't be like Mr. Woak. If you are not ethical, your students will not trust you fully, and if they don't trust you, you will never have much synergy in your classes. Here is how the relationship proceeds:

ETHICS lead to . . .TRUST, which is necessary for . . .SYNERGY

Would I ever have wanted to approach Mr. Woak after the way he treated me? Would I have wanted to talk informally with him? You may have had similar experiences with teachers. If so you probably still harbor ill feelings. All of us from the time we enter school have a strong sense of right and wrong, fairness and justice. That sense is as strong in students who have been mistreated as in those who have been loved and pampered.

Most students hold teachers among the most important adults in their lives, equal to and sometimes above parents. They want to trust teachers. They want them to be caring and helpful and true to their word. They want them to be compassionate, understanding, and loyal—never hurtful or punitive. When teachers show students they will do the right thing consistently, they earn students' trust.

We will not at this point debate whether a teacher must be a genuinely admirable person at heart or whether it is sufficient to present an admirable image to students. I say the important thing is for teachers to show only their good sides to students, even if they do scandalous things outside the classroom. I know what I am saying suggests that teachers should be less than completely truthful, which seems to contradict the ethic of honesty. But we must be realistic. Teachers have the same frailties as all other human beings. I have not known a single one who was perfection personified. We all behave admirably in some circumstances and not so well in others. At times we tell lies, speak disrespectfully, and run others down. Most of us have cheated, at least once or twice in our lives. And not a few of us have done things that bordered on the criminal. But we have also at times (many times, one would hope) been unexpectedly helpful, kind, courteous, generous, honest, and truthful. As said, we are a mix of virtues and vices.

There is a good reason, though, for showing our best face when working with students. Think about this: Would you want to work with someone you knew to be untruthful? Who derided people? Who stole? Who hurt others wantonly? Who had little personal integrity? Do you feel you could develop a trusting relationship with such a person? Similar questions flit about in students' minds. The questions may only occasionally rise to the conscious level, but they are always there somewhere. Students subject teachers to ethical filters and watch to see who passes through and who doesn't.

SEVEN ETHICAL QUALITIES REQUIRED FOR TRUST

To trust a person is to believe that he or she is on your side and will support and not harm you. You are confident you can count on that person. Synergy sometimes occurs in the absence of trust, but only fitfully. It does not develop reliably when you have to work with a person you think will renege on commitments, run you down behind your back, or otherwise do you harm. Students have that reaction to teachers. They will not work closely with us when they feel they cannot trust us.

To make trust possible, teachers must show students they have certain ethical qualities. Those qualities must be shown in teacher behavior, consistently over time. The qualities are not obscure. If we could put them into students' words, they would be something like the following:

1. *Kindness:* Be approachable and treat me and other students well.
2. *Consideration:* Allow me and other students to maintain our self-respect.
3. *Faith:* Show faith in my potential, and in that of other students.
4. *Helpfulness:* Help me and other students learn what we really need or enjoy.
5. *Fairness:* Treat me and other students justly.
6. *Honesty:* Be honest with me and others, but do so tactfully.
7. *Patience:* Be very patient with me. Be patient with other students, too.

Of these principles, kindness, consideration, fairness, and honesty are valued in almost all dealings among individuals. The other three—faith in potential, helpfulness, and patience—are especially prized in the helping professions such as teaching, counseling, and social work. All seven are required in education. They form the bedrock upon which solid trust can be built. If you hope to enjoy the benefits of synergy, you must convince students you possess these traits. It does no good to tell them how ethical you are. They need to see for themselves.

You as a teacher have the burden of initiating trust. It is not a fifty-fifty proposition between you and students. In the beginning you have no control over the attitudes students bring to school. Some may be liars, thieves, and bullies and may honestly believe those traits help them gain status and success. You can help them replace those beliefs after a while with others that serve them better. But you can do that only if your own ethics are always evident. That gives trust a chance to take hold.

When you first meet new students, you see some who behave attractively. It is natural to try to establish relationships with those students. Others may behave in ways that are unappealing or even distressing. Occasionally you may encounter a student or two so unappealing and vice-ridden you doubt you could ever establish trust, or would ever want to. Your natural inclination is to keep your distance from those students. But if you do so, you limit the trust that allows synergy to bloom. Therefore, put it in your mind that you will do your level best to establish trust with every single student, not just those who please you. Getting students with bad-behavior reputations involved in synergy—is one of teaching's great challenges and greatest rewards. That is the way you need to look at it.

Know, too, that students won't see trust from the same perspective as you do. They've probably never heard of synergy or know anything of its value and so are not thinking of trust as helpful to their education. They are concerned first and foremost about protecting themselves, individually. While you are concerned about the whole class, each individual student worries about what sort of treatment you and the other students will dish out. Their initial goal is to keep themselves safe. Concerning you, they have a single question in mind: How is this teacher going to treat me? At first, Juana does not require that you treat all students kindly, but only that you treat her so. Once she sees that you treat her well, she will become concerned about how you treat other students, too. If Juana sees you treat Ramón caustically, she may not become particularly upset, but you will have planted a seed of doubt in her mind. She wonders if you might sometime treat her as you have treated Ramón. For students, initial trust comes from being treated well, individually and collectively.

Remember, your task is to develop trusting relationships with as many of your students as possible, ideally all of them. This will put you on course toward synergy. But if you are loved by several and disliked by several, your classes will not go as you wish and you will not have a happy life in teaching. The negativism, apathy, and recalcitrance of those who do not trust you will obviate the synergy you might otherwise enjoy.

DISPLAYING THE ETHICAL PRINCIPLES THAT LEAD TO TRUST

In this chapter you will see a list of seven ethical principles that lead to trust (Figure 2.1). Those are the principles you must live by, at least in school, and from which you must never waver. Let's take a closer look at these principles and identify specific behaviors that show students our trustworthiness. Students, by the way, are ever watchful for these behaviors in their teachers.

Kindness   This ethic is expressed in the Golden Rule. You can't go wrong if you treat students with **courtesy and respect**—in other words, pretty much as you would like them to treat you. Students want you to acknowledge them, call them by name, and chat with them occasionally. They want you to treat them gently, with a smile. They want you to show them respect by being polite and courteous. They definitely do not want you to scold, yell at them, call them names, intimidate, or punish. Remember: While many acts of kindness go into building trust, a single unkind act from you can destroy it.

Consideration   Many authorities have tried to explain why students behave badly in school. A number of them believe it is because students fail to find acceptance there. They say everyone has a strong desire to belong and to be accepted as a valued member of the group. When acceptance does not come easily, students strive all the harder and some of their efforts fall outside the bounds of acceptable behavior. While there is some truth in that view, most class misbehavior comes from two other causes, neither of them psychologically profound. The first is that students **hate boredom** and **like to have fun**. They want to talk, laugh, and move about. They want to tease their neighbor and make funny faces and noises. These are innocuous behaviors, but can be disruptive in the classroom. Teachers naturally try to suppress them. In fact, most wear themselves out trying to keep a cover on them throughout the day.

The second main cause of classroom misbehavior is tied up with students trying to **maintain personal dignity**. Dignity refers to self-respect and involves sense of one's competence, power, control, and self-direction. We show consideration for students when we do not intrude, without invitation, into their inner lives, when we accept them as they are. The self is fragile. When it is threatened, we throw up shields to protect it, to save face. We don't want anything to make us look stupid, so we avoid situations that might. We would rather lie and cheat than appear incompetent and will often feign indifference rather than involve ourselves in something we're afraid we can't handle. Avoidance of failure is a powerful human motive.

Putting student dignity under threat is a sure way to kill trust. That is why we must always be considerate of students' needs and their ways of coping. Students do not want us to belittle them, ever, for any reason. They do not want us to speak to them sarcastically or use a threatening tone. They want us never to dominate them in confrontations or back them into a corner. They want us to ensure that other students see them succeed, not fail.

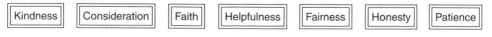

Figure 2.1 Seven ethical principles that build trust

Faith   Students react to school in different ways. Some like it and are successful. Most accept whatever is set before them and try to make do. Some dislike it but prefer to make no waves. A good many just float about. They more or less muddle through and some get lost, educationally, never having come to trust teachers. They may feel worthless and act accordingly, declining to participate in activities, doing little of the assigned work, and behaving insolently.

These students almost never experience what every one of us wants, which is for **somebody to believe in us**, to consider we have worth at present and potential to be better. The young desperately want that from parents and in school they want it from their teachers. They want you to show interest in them, stick with them and tell them you are glad they are in your class. They want you to mention progress they have made. They want you to envision rosy possibilities for their future. When they get that, they feel you believe in them and begin to trust you. When they do not get that acknowledgment, trust never develops. We simply will not trust people who do not believe in us or who, for some reason, fail to show it.

Helpfulness   Helpfulness is a powerful ethic for building trust. Students in school don't think of helpfulness in grand terms, such as being successful in life. They see it in small personal things: helping the kindergartner put on his coat, helping the fourth grader find a misplaced book, and getting another pencil for the seventh grader who has broken hers. They see it when the teacher helps them write uppercase and lowercase letters properly, explains privately how fractions are divided, or cheerfully shows for the third time how to sequence paragraphs to make compositions flow. And they especially see it when teachers help them in troubling situations. "Justin, I know you didn't intentionally break the window. I'll take care of that with the principal." Or "Desiree, I know the assignment you turned in is not entirely your own work. I suspect you felt you couldn't do it on your own. Let me see if I can make a few suggestions so you can do work you'll be proud of." Or "Sara, I could tell that what Alicia and Connie did hurt your feelings. Sometimes people do that without thinking. By the way, I was wondering: Could you stay for a few minutes and help me get these plants watered?"

Fairness   The young have a keen sense of fairness and want it to prevail. Gerry Spence says, "(Children) know when they are being wrongfully repressed. They know right from wrong and they have a nearly perfect sense of justice." (1995, p. 240) Students eagerly call attention to what they perceive as unfairness, especially when they are involved in it. Teachers get tired of that in a hurry, and when students' voices become whiney with, "That's not *fair*," teachers want to retort (and sometimes do), "The world is not a fair place, honey. Get a grip." As if such a comment would immediately set things right in that student's mind.

We miss an opportunity to encourage trust when we dismiss students' concerns about fairness and disregard their complaints. But what does being fair mean? Some say it means treating everyone the same. Others disagree, among them Richard Curwin and Allen Mendler (1988). They believe the fairest, most justifiable position is treating students in accordance with individual needs. Stephen R. Covey, author of *The Seven Habits of Highly Effective People* (1989), takes a similar view. He writes that when dealing with others we should try ". . . to understand them deeply as individuals, the way (we) would want to be understood, and then to treat them in terms of that understanding." (p. 192)

These are convincing points of view. If we truly want to be fair to students, we need to treat them in accordance with the circumstances at a given time and with what we have learned of their needs, backgrounds, and predispositions. We need to explain this rationale to them so they understand exactly what we are doing. Even then differential treatment will occasionally upset students and their parents. In advising teachers how to respond to parents who might complain about unequal treatment their child has received, Richard Curwin (1992) suggests saying the following: ". . . I will be glad to listen to any suggestions you have. . . . However . . . please do not ask me to treat your child just like everybody else. Your child deserves a lot better than that." (pp. 74—75, abridged)

Teachers who are working at establishing trust should be up front about fairness. In language suited to the age of the students, they can say: "I will always try to treat you as fairly as possible and will help you treat each other the same. Sometimes one of you might be treated differently from another. When that happens, it is because of differences I see in the situation or your feelings. But I will always try for fairness. When I fail in that, or anyone in the class fails, it is important that we discuss it." Most students, once the "fair does not mean equal" concept is explained to them, see the justice in it.

Honesty   Teachers want students to tell the truth, and students expect the same of teachers. Despite students' willingness to lie (eagerness, some say), they will not trust a teacher they consider dishonest. To students, verbal honesty means three things: The first is absence of deceit. An honest person does not set out to mislead another. You are not deceitful when you say what you believe to be true, but later find out you have been mistaken. The second meaning of verbal honesty is keeping our promises. If we make promises, we keep them unless prevented by forces outside our control. We don't later hem and haw and say, "Well, I didn't really mean that." The third meaning involves telling things as they actually are. Without embellishment, we tell what really happened or how we really feel. Embellishments make stories convincing and entertaining, but they distort the truth.

Life teaches us that honesty usually *is* the best policy. When we behave honestly, we look better to others *and to ourselves*, even when we have to admit we made a mistake or failed at something. Making mistakes is always acceptable, even useful when we learn from them and thus improve. Any embarrassment associated with confessing a true mistake will be short-lived. But deceit is another matter. It destroys trust and is never forgotten. Who among us has not learned firsthand of the tangled webs we weave when first we practice to deceive? We usually get caught in those webs and dangle there feeling the spider is about to pounce. People we deceive do not excuse us, and they have memories like elephants.

Why, then, do we lie when honesty works best? We may lie to take advantage of another. We may lie to get out of doing a task we find distasteful. We may lie to make ourselves look better or just because it is fun to make stories grander than they really are. Often we lie to avoid the consequences of what we have done. We hope we may fool other people so they won't be angry or take reprisal against us. (We seldom fool them, though, and that invariably gets us deeper into hot water.) We frequently lie to keep from looking incompetent or ignorant. We hate to appear inept and so go through surprising machinations to protect ourselves. Avoiding consequences and protecting our dignity: those are the two main reasons why we lie deceitfully.

Most lies we tell are white lies. Lies come in all shades, from white to black. So far we have been speaking of the black lie, or at least the dark gray, the lie that misleads or does disservice to another. The white lie is used to maintain cordial relations and to flatter. We tell someone how great their scraggly hairdo looks. We tell them how wonderful it is to see them, when all the while we have been trying to avoid them. Teachers have perfected the white lie as an art form. Primary teachers, especially, are forever telling students that their mediocre response is *great!*, that their slipshod work is *super!*, and that their half-hearted efforts show they are *really trying!* They say these things believing they will help students' motivation and self-concept.

White lies probably don't damage trust between teacher and student. But they begin to ring hollow after a time. They mislead students, too. The primary grade examples convey the notion that everything students do is the absolute greatest. But it only takes students a while to see that their poor work is not terrific. That realization doesn't then do a lot for their self-concept. Teachers are more honest when, instead of spreading on superlatives, they acknowledge student improvement and show appreciation for effort. They can enthusiastically say, "Last week you could only do three of these problems, and now you can do them all. That is quite an improvement." Or "You have worked hard on this assignment. I can see the effort you have put into it." When students are not working up to expectations, teachers needn't make them feel bad. They can tactfully say, "We need to get these problems done in the next 10 minutes." Or "I'd like to see you get this work done very neatly. I'll be right here if there is anything I can do to help you."

Patience   Patience might not seem an ethical principle and probably isn't in general. But in teaching it is. The best teachers are enthusiastic and motivating, but they are patient too. They know students work and learn at different speeds. They know that some grasp concepts quickly while others take a while. They know some do their work accurately while others make many mistakes, sometimes over and over. It is very easy to become impatient with students who continually repeat an error. In Spanish class Michael for the fifth time says "*Está listo*" when he should say "*Estoy listo*" to indicate that he is ready. Mr. Rodríguez may feel like saying, "Michael, you got the verb wrong again! This is not hard. Pay attention to what you are saying." But Mr. Rodríguez knows that impatience erodes trust while patience builds it. Instead of speaking exasperatedly, he suggests that Michael try tapping himself on the chest to remember to say *estoy* rather than *está* when referring to himself.

The patient teacher sticks with the student, gives help over and over, and tolerates repeated mistakes, but, of course, tactfully tries to help the student improve. The patient teacher knows that many students make numerous mistakes while learning but may ultimately master the material as well or better than the quicker students. The patient teacher comes to the student's aid over and over and does so pleasantly, never showing exasperation and never putting the student down. It doesn't take students long to learn they can trust that teacher.

PROFESSOR WENDT'S ETHICS AND MY TRUST

Of all the teachers I ever had, Professor Mark Wendt was the one who helped me most. Others might have helped just as much if they'd had the opportunity, but Professor Wendt happened to be in a position to profoundly affect the last two-thirds of my life. He took a stand on my behalf and stood by it. I think he was about as ethical as they come; I never knew him to do anything dishonest or unkind. Certainly, I never had a teacher I trusted more. But what he did that went far beyond anyone else was show faith in me when some powerful people didn't. I suspect he put his neck on the line, though no one ever told me he did. When I first aspired to a career in higher education I was not a sophisticated person. I was semi-book smart but not street smart, word smart but not people smart. I wasn't good at buttering up important people and telling them what they wanted to hear. I was a bit slow in learning jargon and inept in identifying the current politically correct hot topic so I could mention it before anyone else did. Neither was I good at blowing hot air just for pulmonary exercise. Those shortcomings sometimes made me appear inept. In a way I was. A powerful dean at the university was vacillating on whether or not to expend further resources on me, a way of saying he wasn't convinced I was up to snuff, so why keep me around. He had already sent packing another guy that I thought smarter than I. And my major professor in psychology had decided, I then erroneously thought, to withhold his approval too. It looked like my goose was cooked. Farewell to my dreams of ivy encrusted ivory towers. (Sure, I can make light of it *now*. But at that time, believe me—if I'd had a tail, it would have been curled like spring steel between my figurative hind legs.)

I had gotten off to a bad start with the Dean. He had a favorite seminar he taught and I made a presentation in it that didn't exactly thrill him. I committed the sin of talking in practical terms instead of philosophical terms. That alone seemed enough to earn me the kiss of death. Meanwhile, my psychology guy seemed singularly unimpressed with my grasp of cognitive dissonance and other assorted obscurities. From the dissonance that persisted between us you'd have thought I hadn't bathed for six months.

I had been doing some work in a special program under the direction of Professor Wendt. He and I had to travel together three or four hundred miles a week by car. That gave us a lot of time to talk. He frequently asked my opinion about educational matters and seemed to enjoy discussing them with me, and when he learned I could write, he got me to do some editing for him. When my fortunes sank low with the Dean, I told Professor Wendt I would be leaving the doctoral program at the end of the semester. He looked surprised and wanted to know why. I told him. For the first and only time I knew of in all the years we were friends, he used vulgar language to express with concise vehemence what the Dean could do. (Wendt's wife and daughters would have been utterly shocked if they had known.) I didn't know anybody ever spoke that way about the Dean, and I was struck dumb in those less urbane times on hearing my esteemed professor speak in that manner. (I learned then that you could transgress ethics at least once in your professional life.) Professor Wendt told me to forget about the Dean and keep on plugging. He said that if I stayed the course and did what he knew I was capable of, I'd be at the top of the heap before all was said and done. I said I didn't think I had much choice in the matter—the Dean would make the decision for me. Wendt said, "You watch and see." He evidently saw something in me that others didn't. By the time another year rolled around I had the Dean on my side so strongly he was willing to share credit for some of the things I had done, which put a stopper on my ever trusting him again which I didn't anyway. Although we saw each other occasionally in subsequent years and were cordial enough, he was not a person I ever cared to associate with. You can probably understand why.

HOW TRUST IS BUILT, MAINTAINED, AND LOST

If you are to enjoy the benefits of class synergy, you must continually show your personal ethics. As we have seen, you do this through behavior. You may tell students what an honest, patient, and caring person you are, but your words are only words, not the true message. The true message is communicated by your behavior as you interact with students. Don't worry when your students behave unethically. They will do so regularly, at least for a time. Never mind that. Building trust is your responsibility, not theirs. You build it by showing your trustworthy qualities over and over. That is how you draw students into trusting relationships. They will gradually respond in keeping with what you show them.

We should note at this point that ethical behavior is not the only quality students want in teachers. They like for you to have a sense of humor, a pleasing nature, good organization, interesting presentational skills, and ability to tell a good story. They like you to be enthusiastic, outgoing, flexible, and nice looking. Older ones think it neat if you drive a sporty car. But at this point we are concerned with what is required for building trust. Humor and storytelling are marvelously useful in teaching, but are not essential for trust.

For some students, trust grows quickly or may already be in place. For others it grows very slowly. It may take weeks or months to become established, and in the process you may have to deal many times with disrespectful behavior. Nevertheless, trust eventually comes if you persevere, even in the most unlikely cases.

How does this happen? Stephen R. Covey (1989) uses a metaphor he calls "the emotional bank account" to help explain the safety level that a person feels in relation to another. His metaphor applies equally to trust. Imagine a bank account that holds trust on deposit, rather than money. As a teacher, you establish a separate account for every one of your students—for Jonathan, Heather, Mirabel, and so on. Only you can make deposits into these accounts and only you can make withdrawals. The account balances grow as you add deposits. You make a deposit in Jonathan's account every time you speak to him in a friendly manner or show kindness, consideration, helpfulness, or patience. The balance in Jonathan's account indicates the amount of trust he has for you at any given time. When the account balance is high (meaning Jonathan's trust in you is high), you and he find you are able to communicate well and work together easily. When the account balances are high for most of your students, trust is sufficient for synergy to occur.

Trust is lost much more easily than gained. You make a withdrawal from Jonathan's account every time you behave toward him in a manner that is unfair, inconsiderate, impatient, dishonest, or harsh. The balance drops quickly. Two or three violations of ethical principle may entirely wipe out Jonathan's account that took you weeks to build. If you let his account go into the red, it will probably never again amount to much.

One of the most difficult things in teaching is to live continually by the ethical principles we have identified. But that must be done if trust is to be maintained. As Covey puts it,

> People will forgive mistakes, because mistakes are usually of the mind, mistakes of judgment. But people will not easily forgive the mistakes of the heart, the ill intention, the bad motives, the prideful justifying cover-up of the first mistake. (1989, p. 199)

In the same manner, students easily excuse mistakes we make when teaching lessons or assigning homework. Those are mistakes of the mind. But they neither excuse nor forget mistakes of the heart, where essential ethical principles are violated.

WHERE DO WE GO FROM HERE?

In Chapter 1 you learned about synergy, how it sometimes occurs in the classroom, and nine elements that you can put in place to make synergy happen. In this chapter we explored the first two of those elements—teacher ethics and trust. We examined seven ethical principles and specific behaviors associated with them, and we have seen how trust is built, maintained, and lost. We move next to consider the element of charisma, what it is, why students like it, and how you can increase your appeal to students.

TO THINK ABOUT

1. Seven teacher traits, based on ethical principles, were identified as essential in developing trust with students: kindness, consideration, faith, helpfulness, fairness, honesty, and patience. Which of these traits would you consider most important for trust? Which would be least important? Could any of them be left out?
2. Think back to a teacher you had whom you would now consider highly ethical. What did that teacher do, and not do, that seemed ethical? Did that teacher behave in accord with all seven ethical principles?
3. Think back to a teacher you had whom you disliked. Is your dislike linked to one or more of the seven ethical principles? If so, which of the principles was violated?

4. Analyze your personal behavior with regard to the ethical principles that build trust. Are there any in which you might improve your behavior toward students? What specifically might you work on?
5. Suppose you have a student in class who is bad-tempered and bad-mannered. You need to build trust with him. How will you do so?

3

CHARISMA: HOW TO CAST YOUR MAGIC SPELL

Ms. Postlethwaite, you know the class pet squirrel you let us take care of over the weekend... well, we were wondering if there are any limits to your unconditional love for us?

MAGGIE CLARK'S FIRST GRADE

It is a marvelous thing to see Maggie Clark work with first grade students. Little tots naturally love their teachers, but Maggie has something special. You see it in many ways: Students cluster around her. She hardly ever has a discipline problem. Students still consider they belong to her after they leave first grade. Somewhere along the way they become her friends. Many drop by to see her after they are in middle school. Not a few decide once in college to become teachers, another tribute to Maggie's influence. They like to talk with her about teaching and help in her classroom to get the feel for it. They enjoy telling the children they were once Mrs. Clark's students. They like to relate stories about nice things that happened when they were in her room. Three or four of Maggie's former students now teach in the same school system with her. They enjoy hanging around her just as they did years before.

Maggie has natural charisma. She attracts people at first sight, both children and adults, but especially children. Little kids in restaurants and shopping malls stare at her. When she smiles at them, they smile back. I've never been able to understand exactly why. I don't have those experiences myself. Maggie is an attractive woman, but that is not the reason. You see beautiful women and handsome men that little children barely notice. There is something else, in her eyes maybe, that says she is interested in them and approachable.

If people's initial reaction to Maggie intrigues me, so does what comes later. Attraction is one thing. Some people are born with it. But though it establishes contact, it doesn't necessarily lead further. For Maggie it does. Give her a couple of minutes and she'll wrap any kid around her finger. I have seen her do it in and out of the classroom. She says she doesn't know why children like her right off, but she admits she does cultivate them after that. Now that she has told me what she does, it is easy enough to see.

When Maggie meets a young child she speaks to him or her. She smiles and looks right in the child's face and says hello. She continues to smile. The kid might or might not reply but always looks back at her and doesn't try to get away. If the child is old enough to talk, Maggie asks, "What is your name?" She then asks, "How old are you?" "Is that a new dress (or shirt or shoes)?" "Where's mommy?" "Do you have a brother or sister? What are their names? Where are they now?" For older kids she asks, "What have you been doing today? How has the day been going?" And so on. Kids stand there and answer her questions and before you know it they are offering information on their own. Maggie tells them her name, too, and says something like, "I've just been to the grocery store. Have you ever been in that large one on State Street?" Maggie says she talks with children because it's fun. People of all ages interest her. She likes to learn about their lives. She is a true expert at opening them up. I envy that. Just watching her has helped me become better at it.

There is more to the process than Maggie tells, probably more than she knows. People with natural talent often can't explain exactly what they do. Maggie thinks she attracts people because she finds them fascinating. But why would that be attractive? My guess: Genuine fascination emanates from her somehow and others pick up on it. That is the part I can't nail down. The rest of what she does is learnable and doable. Take people's names, for example. Myself, I'm sort of reluctant to ask people their names even though I have read that a person's own name is the sweetest sound they ever hear. I don't think anybody told Maggie that, but whenever she meets a stranger she learns their name right away and repeats it frequently while talking with them. Kid, adult, or corporate CEO, it doesn't matter. They remember her for doing it.

Maggie goes further than names, though. She remembers what people divulge about themselves. When she sees them again, she asks about what they told her previously. Then she learns something new and remembers it and asks about it next time. She knows that the best way to get people interested in you is to become genuinely interested in them. Maggie passes that information along to her first graders. She always tells and shows them that the best way to have a friend is to be a friend.

THE NATURE AND POWER OF CHARISMA

Teacher charisma is one of the nine elements that contribute to class synergy. Charisma is a quality we possess that draws others to us. It is usually likened to magnetism; in fact, it is often called animal magnetism. But charismatic magnetism isn't physical; it is psychological. Certain people attract us and we want to be near them, listen to them, follow them, and pay attention to what they do. They don't have to be beautiful. They don't have to be eloquent. They don't have to be rich. They don't have to be showmen, daredevils, great writers, or performers. Some very charismatic people can't lay claim to any of those traits. They nevertheless attract followers, sometimes in multitudes. How do they do it? More importantly for us, how can teachers do it?

A few of us don't need to develop charisma at all. We already have it in abundance. A few of us have almost none and are resigned to compensating for the lack of it in other ways. Most of us are in the middle; we have some but not as much as we'd like. You have had teachers who delighted you. You have had others who were knowledgeable and well organized but so wooden they couldn't charm a fly off the wall. Though charisma is very important for teachers, it is not talked about much in education. We have the wrong idea about it. We think it is static, that it doesn't change, that we either have it or not, like wavy hair or smooth skin. What an unfortunate misconception. Charisma is not a fixed trait. It is malleable. Qualities that comprise charisma can be learned and improved.

Lots of teachers claim they are not charismatic but are good teachers. They may be correct on both counts. But the chances are their classes rarely if ever experience synergy. Their students may work well, behave well, and learn a considerable amount, yet never taste the exhilaration of doing high-quality work in an energized ambiance. That kind of education would bring them running back for more. Solid non-charismatic teaching can keep classes functioning well, but if they ever reach the energized level it is by accident. That fact was overlooked by educators who pushed for programmed learning back in the 1970s. It was believed then that students could learn by themselves at their own pace from printed material. No teacher was needed. The material led students step-by-step to so-called mastery. In actual practice, students didn't like programmed learning and those subjected to it mastered almost nothing. The only people who liked it were those who wrote the darned stuff.

While we don't understand the central essence of charisma, we know a good deal about what charismatic teachers do. We can learn to approach people and draw them to us as Maggie Clark does. We can learn to pep up our personality, put our best self forward, and intrigue people with our special talent, experience, and knowledge. All these things increase charisma. In order to make ourselves more attractive, we have only to put them to use.

THE TWO PHASES OF CHARISMA

Charisma occurs in two phases—an **attraction phase** and a **fulfillment phase.** The two can be likened to a meal presented by a cordon bleu chef. In the attraction phase, the food is presented in colors that contrast brilliantly, in textured layers. The aromas make you swoon. You can't wait to try it. But the meal is no good if it doesn't fulfill its promise. Imagine your reaction if the sauce is too salty, the viand unchewable, or the vegetables watery. The same is true with charisma. Some people have charismatic qualities that make our hair stand on end, but for some reason leave us with no sense of fulfillment. When you decide to charm your students, you'll want to make sure you can provide some substance, too.

Have you ever attended one of those seminars where a speaker tells you in an hour or two how to make a fortune in real estate? Those speakers make abundant use of charismatic devices—eye-catching dress, dramatic delivery, anecdotes galore, a joke every 30 seconds. With their charm they get you to devour the "true" stories of incredible success. At the end of the seminar you are full of pep and eager to make your first million, which you expect by next month. Disillusionment, though, awaits. The get-rich-quick strategy you have bought might work for an occasional person, but I've never known anybody who benefited from it. Myself, I once sank $300 into a seminar and never made a penny from what I learned. But you know what? I consider the money well spent. It taught me a thirty-thousand-dollar lesson and only cost three hundred. A genuine bargain any day of the week.

I sometimes watch get-rich presentations on television and attend seminars in person, provided I can get in free. They have taught me much about charisma and how to use it, especially in the attraction phase. However, they don't provide much fulfillment, which is what the presentation is supposed to be about. A minor detail conveniently forgotten. While the seminars have taught me almost nothing about fulfillment, they have indirectly made me learn a lot. They made me think through what would have to come next if those presenters were teachers in charge of ongoing classes day after day. They couldn't get by with making students all excited and then dropping them. They'd have to deliver the goods.

Most teachers are skilled at delivering the educational goods over the long run, provided their students cooperate. But student cooperation—therein lies the rub. If teachers are not sufficiently charismatic, they cannot rally students to learning. They never move their classes into synergy that lets them run with the ball. Without synergy, teaching and learning move like draft horses instead of racehorses. How much better it is when we excite students and make them eager for learning. If you do that day after day, your students will work with you and even revere you, as they do Maggie Clark and Violet Cooper.

THE ATTRACTION PHASE

In the 1930s, philosopher and educator John Dewey began urging teachers to motivate students and give them a more active role in learning. He believed active involvement helped students construct knowledge, whereas sitting and listening all too often put them to sleep or made them wish they were elsewhere. Ever since Dewey's time, teachers have been told it is essential to "motivate" their students. They are to indicate in lesson plans how they will get students interested and make lessons meaningful. Everybody agrees students don't learn when not interested or unable to see the point. But distressingly, despite the ubiquitous attention to motivation, student *disinterest* predominates in a great proportion of today's classrooms. It is more the rule than the exception. In Chapter 5 we will see how to redress that condition. But for now, suffice to say that charismatic teachers do not bore their students to death. They have a knack for making dull topics palatable. When they can't, they use their personality to liven things up, and when that doesn't work they toss the lesson out in favor of something else.

Virtually all teachers can increase their charisma. They can do it genuinely. No fakery is needed–no illusions, no deceit, no magic. It's easy: Look closely at what charismatic people do and teach yourself the same. You won't become a robotic copy of them. Your own traits will combine with what you learn to form your unique style. To help with this process, try focusing on the following: (1) What you show in your outer personality, (2) Your way of talking with students, (3) Sharing information about your personal life, (4) Relating and capitalizing on personal experiences, (5) Sharing your special skills, (6) Sharing your special knowledge, and (7) Presenting yourself memorably. You have most of this stuff already inside you. You only need to transfer it from your inner to your outer personality.

Your Outer Personality

Our personality is shown in how we act. People are said to have a bubbly personality or a cynical personality or a moody personality or a bland personality. Psychologists consider personality to be the totality of one's thoughts and behaviors. They say everything we do and think, however minute, is part of our personality. They are no doubt correct, but we can't know much about people's inner feelings and thoughts. For that reason it is helpful to think of our having two personalities, separate but related—an **inner personality** and an **outer personality.** The inner personality is kept private; the outer personality is shown to others.

The outer personality is what teachers let their students see. Their inner personality may be bland, but they don't have to let anybody in on the secret. Their outer personality tells others everything they need to know. It does this through facial expressions, friendliness, enthusiasm, bodily carriage, sense of humor, wit, compassion, sensitivity to others, and manner of speaking. From time to time students are asked what they like in teachers. Young students say they like teachers who are "nice." By that they mean friendly and caring, with smiles and kind words. Older students say they like teachers who are friendly, witty, interesting, and patient. They like their teachers to be engaging, enjoy a joke, see the humor in situations, and liven up things. We can benefit from paying attention to what students like.

Smiles and Bodily Carriage   Students are attracted to teachers who smile and whose bodily carriage says they are sure of themselves. Forget that stuff about beginning with a gruff demeanor. That's no good. You want to draw students to you, not push them away. Walk with confidence. Hold your head up. If you are not a natural smiler, practice it. Look your students in the face and give them a group smile and many individual personal smiles. Spread them around. There is an old Chinese proverb that says "A man without a smiling face must not open a shop." The proverb, written before gender awareness, applies to teachers as well as shopkeepers. Teachers without a smiling face should not open a classroom. Dale Carnegie (1981) tells of a sign about smiles that appeared in a department store at Christmastime. It included the following:

> A smile costs nothing, but creates much.
> It enriches those who receive without impoverishing those who give.
> It happens in a flash and the memory of it may last forever.
> It is of no earthly good to anybody until it is given away.

The easiest thing in the world is to smile. If you are not a natural smiler, learn how to do it engagingly. You can practice in secret. Smiles just make everything go better.

Friendliness   Just as we can learn to make better use of smiles, so can we learn to be more friendly with students. The best way to begin is to learn and use their names quickly. Ask how they are and how things are going for them. Show you are glad they are in your class. You may think there is not time for you to do all this, but every minute you spend on it saves at least two you'd have to waste dealing with misbehavior and it leaves good feelings, not bad ones. You don't have to speak with every student every day. But you can make eye contact with every student and smile. Spread the friendly talk around so each student gets some of it occasionally. Imagine how you would react to a teacher who treated you that way instead of speaking to you only when you did something wrong.

Enthusiasm   Students gravitate to teachers who are enthusiastic. They shy away from those who are not. Misery may love company, but students don't love misery. Contrast the dreary teacher with one who shows enthusiasm for the subject, topic, students, and life in general. Enthusiasm enlivens everyone. Of course, it has to be genuine. You can't with a dead expression say how really exciting the spelling lesson is going to be and expect students to leap in pell-mell. You've got to act like you believe it—and then you'll have to make it so. We can learn how to show enthusiasm. We should practice it every day. It will make our personality shine. Even when our inner personality is down in the dumps, we can put zest into our outer personality and do ourselves a favor in the process. Behavioral psychologists tell us our outer behavior usually affects our inner feelings. If we act enthusiastic, we can actually begin to feel enthusiastic.

Sensitivity and Compassion   Sensitivity and compassion are related. A *sensitive* person is affected by impressions received from others. Sensitive teachers pick up on how students are feeling. We can tell when a student has had trouble, perhaps at home or with another student. We can tell when the class is bored or laboring. We recognize our students' feelings and deal with the situation as best we can. We don't pretend nothing is wrong and plow on ahead no matter what. *Compassion* means we have pity for someone or sympathy for them. We can relate to what has happened to our students and how they are feeling. When students have disturbing experiences they appreciate compassionate teachers. They don't expect you to solve their problems, but they want your sympathy and understanding. What should you do when you see they are troubled? Ask them privately if something is bothering them and if they'd like to talk about it. If they want to talk, arrange a time and private place. If they decline, don't pry. Tell them you are available to listen if they feel like talking.

Your Way of Talking with Students
You read how Maggie Clark speaks with people and how she affects them. Perhaps you already have an easy approachable way with people, as she does. If you don't, you can learn to speak with students in ways that open them up to you. Look them in the face, smile, say hello, call them by name, and ask how they are. They will respond, usually by returning your smile. That is the way to begin. Try making a point of greeting your students regularly in this way. Make sure everybody, not just your favorites, gets a personal word from you.

When you chat with your students, learn something about them. Never be condescending. Show you are interested by giving them genuine attention. No need to pretend where this is concerned. They will tell you about themselves and their interests. Be a good listener and remember what they say. You don't need to reveal much about yourself. When you let them talk, they become more attracted to you. This happens because by listening you make the student feel appreciated. Everybody wants that; in fact, they crave it. Students in class often act out hoping to convince others of their importance. Let each student know he or she is important to you and to the class. You make them feel that way by how you talk to them and even more by how you listen.

Telling about Your Personal Life

We have just said that when talking with students you don't need to tell them much about yourself. But a little produces nice results. It helps them see you as a real person rather than an anchorless spirit that drifts to school at dawn and fades away at dusk. Students of all ages want to know if you have a spouse, significant other, children, or pets. They like to see photos of them and know what you do on outings. They are eager to know about your hobbies and favorite foods, movies, and television programs. These are things they relate to. It opens their eyes to discover you like and enjoy some of the same things they do.

Don't give them big doses of your private life. A brief overview is enough. You can add more information from time to time. If your spouse is receiving an award, tell something about him or her and how proud you are. If a school vacation is coming up, mention something you intend to do or maybe recall a memorable vacation you once had. If your pet has to go to the vet, tell about it in a way that makes the animal seem real. If you like to garden, tell what you are planting and why. These bits of personal information intrigue your class and help reduce the distance between you and them. If they ask personal questions that cut into instructional time, assure them you will tell them more as days pass but that it is now time to get down to business.

Telling about Unusual Experiences

All of us have had experiences others find fascinating. Students enjoy hearing about yours. You may have worked at a variety of jobs. Maybe you were a guide in a regional or national park. Maybe you have traveled nationally or to foreign lands. Maybe you have worked on an American Indian reservation, in an inner city, or on a wheat farm. Students love to hear about it. If you have collected memorabilia, share some of it occasionally. Paul, who lived in Brazil, sometimes shows color slides and plays Brazilian music. Elena spent time in Australia and tells about kangaroos, koalas, boomerangs, and aboriginal people. William went on an extended vacation in Alaska and learned about Eskimos, glaciers, and sled dogs. Marcia went on a Carribean cruise, visited a number of port cities, and passed through the Panama Canal. Such experiences, perhaps mundane to you, are fascinating to students.

Sharing Special Skills

Mr. Anderson, my teacher in fourth-grade, always kept a model airplane on his desk. We boys were wild about the models and wanted to crowd around and touch them. I can't remember the girls' reaction. The models were not replicas of real aircraft but flying models made of balsa wood and tissue paper with rubber-band motors. I remember clearly the first day in his class. Mr. Anderson wound the propeller on a little white plane and said, "I don't know where this will go, but if you promise to stay in your seats, I'll let it take off and fly. It will crash into something, maybe one of you, but it won't hurt you. Just let it fall. Let me pick it up for now. Later I'll show you how to handle it." We gave our solemn oaths we'd stay put. He let the plane take off from his desk and it flew in a circle and hit the chalkboard on the side of the room. Mr. Anderson retrieved it. He said, "If you like model airplanes, I'll show you how to make them. We could make one together and take it outside and fly it on a still day." We thought that was incredibly swell stuff. It gave Mr. Anderson star status.

Antonio Gaspar, a history teacher I knew, also liked models. He was a railroad buff and collected models of locomotives and rolling stock that had played important roles in American history. He had a locomotive that burned alcohol and generated enough steam from a thimbleful of water to pull two cars and a caboose several times around a track. Mr. Gaspar had a track he could install in minutes. On it he would from time to time place a particular model. He would tell students about it—what the model replicated, when the original was manufactured, where it operated, and what it was used for.

I once knew a sixth grade teacher named Jen Merton. She was near retirement and had hands deformed by arthritis. She had once been a fine pianist and could still play well. She played sometimes for her students, a few minutes at a time. She would include popular tunes along with songs she was teaching the class. When she wanted students to relax she played classical music. Because of pain in her fingers she could no longer perform complicated pieces, but she could beautifully play "Clair de Lune," "Traumerei," and other haunting melodies. The students loved it. Usually they sat quietly and listened. Sometimes, for fun, Mrs. Merton would let them do what they liked best—come up and stand around the piano and sing while she played.

An art teacher I know named Therese Wong loves sculpting. She makes figurines, usually from clay, sometimes from wood, and occasionally from alabaster. Although she doesn't teach sculpting in school, she sometimes shows students how she does her work. She gives them lumps of clay and lets them emulate her. Another art teacher named Alex Butoni is an outstanding cartoonist. He works summers in malls where for a fee he makes cartoon drawings of people. His students love him to render likenesses of them. He does this as a reward for those who try hard. He teaches his students techniques of cartooning and also helps them learn to draw realistically. Students never forget Mr. Butoni.

Sharing Special Knowledge

Just as your special skills can earn instant admiration, so can your special knowledge. Victoria Harrison, a biology teacher, serves as education consultant to a zoo. She has illustrations of unusual animals and sometimes brings small animals to class. Some teachers make a point of keeping up with television programs and movies most popular with their students. Some pay attention to the latest craze in music, so they can discuss performers, concerts, and albums. Students are enthralled when teachers talk knowingly about favorite personalities, characters, and events. Some teachers learn about automobiles and off-road vehicles that intrigue students—they may actually like the vehicles themselves. Others focus on world and national events. They keep a world map posted and every day mark a place where an interesting event is occurring. They sometimes encourage students to learn about the geography of the area and the lifestyles of the people.

Presenting Yourself Memorably

Students usually focus on and remember one or two traits about each of their teachers. It may be hairstyle, mode of dress, use of makeup, or general demeanor. When I was in high school Miss Pctee, librarian, was the classical old maid, plain-faced, hair up in a bun, and dress 15 years out of date. Mrs. Spivey, home economics, was known for her strident gait. Mr. Lemaster, language teacher, was to us a mustachioed Don Juan. Miss Cantelli of natural science was a careless ragamuffin with the strap of her slip always hanging down her sleeve. Mr. Chagnall, drama teacher, was a long-haired, dark, brooding genius. While none of those people should have been characterized as we remembered them, the impressions nevertheless stuck. That would not have been the case if those teachers had given us a chance to know them as people. They didn't (a mistake you won't make). That wasn't how teachers thought they should conduct themselves in those days. When I established social connections with some of them a few years later, I learned they were real people after all, which surprised me.

I have known a few teachers who capitalized on students' inclination to stereotype. They intentionally presented an image by which to be known. Mr. Gastelli wore a vest and cap every day. He varied the colors and fabrics, but the vest and cap were constant. Inside the classroom, the cap always sat on his desk. He told me he did that to establish his identity. It seemed to work. Students liked to hang around him, though I never understood what the vest and cap had to do with it. Maybe they loosened Mr. Gastelli up. Miss Galloway dressed stylishly, moved elegantly, and used impeccable manners. Other teachers might have made unseemly comments about her had not Miss Galloway been so nice to them. She presented herself that way, she said, to show students there was value in gentility and etiquette. She hoped some of the girls might emulate her. They didn't often get exposed to manners, she maintained. Mr. Romero, a Spanish teacher, wore a beret and always said a word or phrase in Spanish to students he met in the corridor or on the grounds. He wanted them to think Spanish when they saw him. Lots of them, he claimed, considered Spanish just a dull school subject rather than a language real people spoke. Students got a kick out of him, and he was able to get lots of them to say a word or two back in Spanish. That pleased him. One primary teacher I knew, Jeanette Oliver, delivered her self-styled image via a special corner in the room. She had her desk there, with a display of photographs of her husband, two children, two big white dogs, and three Siamese cats. On the shelves were some puzzles and storybooks children liked. On the floor behind the shelves, screened off from the class but open to her chair and desk, was a piece of carpet with two large pillows on it. Sometimes she invited students as a treat to come sit in the special corner and play with the puzzles, look at books, or do their work there. The things they remembered best about the charismatic Ms. Oliver were how nice she was and how much they liked sitting in her special corner.

THE FULFILLMENT PHASE

We noted that your charisma attracts students and predisposes them to cooperate with you. We said your charisma occurs in two phases: initial attraction and fulfillment. Up to this point we have explored the attraction phase. That is what you start off with so students want to associate with you and follow where you lead. Now let's assume you've made yourself irresistible and your students are dying to learn. You don't want to lose the magic moment. What do you do? Answer: you meet their **surface expectations** as well as their **subsurface expectations.** Their surface expectation—what they know they want—is for you to remain attractive. They don't want you to be a shining star the first week and a dud thereafter. Their subsurface expectation, which they don't think about much though they consider it important, is for you to deliver the educational goods. They want you to teach them knowledge and skills they need. Let's explore what you can do to fulfill those expectations.

Meeting the Surface Expectations

On the surface, students want you to be, and to remain, charismatic. They like you to cheer them up and make them feel better. You like that yourself—it's a big change from the ordinary for most of us. To meet this expectation you continue to radiate friendliness, enthusiasm, and good humor. You smile at students and talk with them individually.

You intrigue them with information about yourself—your personal life, your experiences and your expertise.

In addition, you need to provide what we'll call **professional love.** Swallow hard and have a go at showing unconditional love for all your students. Call it care or concern if love doesn't seem to be the right word. Show it to every single student. That doesn't mean you get teary-eyed over them. It means you steadfastly do all you can to help them learn and feel secure and appreciated. You must do this at every opportunity, even when they don't act nice, when they don't try and when they talk back. This is not easy to do, obviously. It is not a natural response. But there is a successful way to approach it. You simply tell yourself, and *mean* it, that you will do your best for them, regardless. You refuse to take their rudeness personally (yes, this is very difficult). You don't scold or fight with them. You know you are doing everything you can to help them. What more could you do? If you keep your equanimity and continue trying sincerely and don't allow yourself to harangue or lecture, you will get a marvelous surprise: One day the naughty students will begin to like you. Even those you considered hopeless. Stephen R. Covey has written eloquently about giving unconditional love:

> . . . when we truly love others without condition, without strings, we help them feel secure and safe and validated and affirmed in their essential worth, identity, and integrity. Their natural growth process is encouraged. We make it easier for them to live the laws of life—cooperation, contribution, self-discipline, integrity—and to discover and live true to the highest and best within them. (1989, p. 199)

Giving professional love unconditionally requires several things of you. We've talked about some of them. You have to understand individual students, to get inside their heads and learn what they want and what they fear. You have to extend them little kindnesses and courtesies, continually, over and over. You have to remain approachable. You have to avoid scolding, lecturing, and punishing. Your worst-acting students are the ones who benefit most. They may act rude and uncaring but they are sensitive and vulnerable, every bit as much as students who behave well. You have to keep your commitments to them, those you have expressed aloud and those you've made silently. You can't throw up your hands and quit. You've got to keep moving ahead. And always, no matter what, you show your personal integrity—your ethics, your resolve, your reliability, your self-discipline. You do all this with a smile. Or if a smile is not appropriate, with a kindly expression. You'll like yourself for it, and you will be surprised how much pressure it takes off you.

Meeting the Subsurface Expectations
In addition to surface expectations, students have other educational expectations they seldom think of consciously. They are naturally optimistic, at

least to begin with. They expect school to be good for them and teach them something worthwhile. They fully expect its benefits to outweigh the inconvenience of being stuck there. Many lose that expectation after a few years. At the middle and high school levels, half or more no longer believe school will offer them anything worthwhile. They see so little value in what they are asked to do, they don't consider it worth trying. They have lost hope and must regain it if they are to learn.

Four things will turn that picture around. You can easily provide all of them. The first is to let students learn some things they truly **want to know.** Never mind whether we consider the topics valuable. Only occasionally do students get that opportunity in school. Their interests don't often match what we think they ought to learn. That makes it incumbent on us to examine critically what we offer them. Do they really need what we are teaching? Do they want it at all? It won't do any harm to find out. Within the parameters of a given subject, ask students what they'd like to know and what they'd find useful. They may not have many ideas at first, so you can be prepared to suggest some. Let them think about it. They will guide you and will appreciate your concern.

The second thing is to make sure we provide learning that is **interesting and useful.** Everything we feel obliged to teach ought to be made interesting and we ought to check to make sure it is useful. If students find learning interesting, good. If they find it useful, that's better. If they find it both interesting and useful, that's the best. They have probably never thought about what happens to a person who lives for several months weightless in space. They probably don't know when baby bears are born or what size they are at birth. They talk about strange sounding accents but probably have never considered what causes accents and dialects. They probably can't identify household products that are poisonous and don't know what to do if one is ingested. They've all heard of cancer but probably don't know what it is, how it harms us, or what forms it takes. They may have seen a performer demonstrate incredible feats of memory but have no idea how we remember things or improve our memories.

The third thing that will change students' minds about learning is to make sure they **have fun** in the process. They'll learn boring material if they can enjoy themselves while doing so, if they can talk and work with others and do creative things and share them. They just don't like to sit still, be quiet, and get the spark of life bored out of them. In Chapter 5 we'll see what teachers can do to make learning more enjoyable.

The fourth thing that can make students change their mind about learning is for you to **energize them.** That's what we are getting at in this book. If you are ethical they will trust you; if you are charismatic they will follow you and try to please you; and when you bring the class up to synergy, they will experience pleasure in learning they haven't known since first grade. Not always, but often enough. When they like and admire you and believe you are going all out for them, they will cooperate with you on most anything you ask.

The way to maintain charisma, once you have gained students' initial interest, is to show that you will bust your tail for them, that you will help them learn things that are important, interesting, and useful to their lives, and that you will do your best to help them have an enjoyable time while doing so. If you do those things and avoid damaging students' trust, they will give back to you the best they have.

Where Do We Go from Here?

We continue examining the elements that contribute to synergy. You have become mindful of showing only ethical behavior to students, and from that beginning have learned how to build up trust. Given the foundation of trust, you have begun putting the other elements of synergy in place. This chapter has dealt with charisma, which is under your control and entirely your responsibility. We will move next to communication. There we will learn about communicating effectively in the classroom, about what to say and not to say to students, how to confer dignity through communication, how to set up formal venues for communication, and how all this ultimately contributes to synergy.

To Think About

1. One of the great benefits teachers enjoy is receiving a regular paycheck no matter how well they teach. Some deserve 10 times what they are paid. A few deserve half or less. Suppose your students can enroll in any class they want, and that your pay is based on the number of students whose parents select you as their child's teacher. In other words, you depend on your reputation to attract students. If that were the case, would you change anything about the way you teach and/or interact with students? If so, what would it be? (If you are not yet teaching, list 10 things you would do to build a sparkling reputation.)
2. Who was the most charismatic teacher you ever had? How did you relate to that teacher? Did you like him or her? Who was the least charismatic you can remember? What did he or she do that left that impression?
3. Many teachers would like to be more charismatic but feel they are not naturally inclined that way and cannot change their basic personality. To what extent do you agree with them? Do you think basic personality can change at all? Do you think teachers can show an outward personality that is different from their inner personality? Do you think they should?

4

COMMUNICATION: WHERE WORDS ARE WORTH MORE THAN A THOUSAND PICTURES

Miss Alonzo searched frantically for the best means of helping Marty at the precise moment, but her mind boggled.

Your desire is to be an effective, energized teacher. You want students to rally to your side, cooperate with each other, enjoy the class, and treat everyone with consideration. You may even dream of teaching without having to contend with misbehavior. Most teachers would think that dream unrealistic, but I hope by now you are convinced it's not. You are steadily moving toward its fulfillment as you display ethical behavior, establish trust, and make yourself charismatically attractive. We will now see how communication can take you a step further.

To a surprising degree, how you communicate determines your effectiveness as a teacher. Relationships are built on communication and are easily destroyed by it. You may think words are just words, messages just messages, and directions just directions. But the proper word at the proper time can ignite synergy while the wrong word can bury it. Consider the following scenarios:

1. Shawon and Jerrold are talking in the back of the room during algebra. Everyone is supposed to be working quietly. Mr. Abramson, helping a student at the front, straightens up and looks at them sternly. He says sharply, "Shawon! Jerrold! No talking back there! I don't want to tell you again!" He glares at them after they slump back over their work.

   How do you think Mr. Abramson's comments make Shawon and Jerrold feel? Do you suppose he increased their eagerness to cooperate with him?

2. Raymond and Justin are talking in the back of the room during English. Everyone is supposed to be working quietly. Mr. Berensen, circulating among students at work, eases alongside them and asks quietly, "Do you fellows need some help?" They get back to work without saying anything. Mr. Berensen adds, "If you have difficulty, let me know."

   How do you think that makes Raymond and Justin feel? Would they remain inclined to cooperate with Mr. Berensen?

COMMUNICATION AND SYNERGY

With the exception of trust, no element of synergy is more important than communication. Synergy occurs from the delight and inspiration that sometimes comes with communicative exchange. Note the word "exchange." Information is *imparted* when it goes in a single direction: One person sends it and another person receives it, as is happening to you at this moment. Only occasionally does imparted information lead to synergy. Information is *exchanged* when it goes back and forth interactively between two or more people. This kind of communication often leads to synergy. If you could react to me about what you are reading right now, with observations, questions, and suggestions, and I could respond to you, our excitement would double or treble.

In most classes, teachers do too much imparting and not enough exchanging. They believe it is inefficient to spend time on in-depth interaction with students. But such exchanges are actually the most efficient way to promote most kinds of learning. They lead to deeper knowledge while improving relationships and, of course, they energize the teaching-learning process. We don't get far these days by demanding that students sit still, pay attention, and remember what we say. In fact, we don't get far when we demand anything of them.

Many years ago, Haim Ginott provided some of the best advice ever on classroom communication. He began as a school teacher before moving into higher education. At the time of his death at age 51, he was a professor at New York University, a nationally syndicated columnist on personal communication, resident psychologist on the *Today* show, and advisor to UNESCO. Ginott said he learned early in his career that

> I am the decisive element in the classroom. It is my personal approach that creates the climate. It is my daily mood that makes the weather. As a teacher I possess tremendous power to make a child's life miserable or joyous. I can be a tool of torture or an instrument of inspiration. I can humiliate or humor, hurt or heal. In all situations it is my response that decides whether a crisis will be escalated or de-escalated, and a child humanized or de-humanized. (1971, p. 13)

Ginott showed us how to use communication to build students' dignity. He believed the key lay in what teachers say when students make mistakes or behave improperly. When Juan carelessly spills paint on the carpet, how should his teacher react? Should she berate him? Should she remind him sternly that it is the third time he's done it? Should she look exasperated and let Juan stew while she cleans up the mess? These responses are not unusual and all have damaging effects.

Ginott said teacher responses should always address the situation and never the character of the student. When Juan spills the paint, his teacher should only say, "We need to clean that up. Here, let's do it together." In saying that, she addresses the situation. She doesn't remind Juan that he's clumsy or careless, thoughtless or hopeless. She just says, "We need to clean that up." Her facial expression is benign. Her voice carries no hint of exasperation. She doesn't roll her eyes or turn her palms up to heaven. She and Juan just clean up the spill and the class goes on about its business.

Ginott has given us much advice like this. We'll come back for more of it later.

ASPECTS OF CLASSROOM COMMUNICATION

My father-in-law Boyd, now deceased, had an old mantelpiece clock he kept going for over 50 years. Never once in that time did he take it to a clocksmith. It was a windup clock in a curved case and it kept surprisingly good time. Year after year it ticked and chimed the hour and was taken for granted—until it stopped, which it did this every two or three years. When it stopped, Boyd would remove the works from the case, take the hands and face off, fill a bucket with kerosene, and slosh the works around in it. Then he would set the mechanism out to dry and later put everything back together. He said he did that to clean the clock. He thought dust accumulated in the cogs until it jammed everything up. Maybe he was right and maybe the kerosene did clean it, but I believe mostly what it did was lubricate. Running day after day for years the old springs and gears got increasingly dry until they could no longer overcome friction. Mostly all the clock needed was a bit of light oil. I don't know what finally happened to that old clock. I like to think it is still running somewhere and that whoever owns it knows it likes a dose of kerosene now and then.

In many classrooms, communication is like the workings of Boyd's clock. It needs lubrication to keep going and maybe occasionally some cleaning too. The mechanism of classroom communication has seven gears that need to be watched closely. They are listening, understanding, reacting helpfully, encouraging, persuading, disagreeing productively, and resolving problems amicably. In this chapter we will give attention to the first four. (We will attend to the last three in Chapter 9 which deals with problem resolution.) These aspects of communication must be kept positive. They must never produce hurt or mistrust. If we make sure they don't, we can keep our classes ticking as reliably as Boyd's old clock.

Listening

Years ago, those of us in teaching talked a great deal about the importance of listening but that was about all we did—talk. In 1973 I received the best lesson on listening I ever had. It came from Carl Rogers, the famous psychologist who popularized client-centered therapy. I had read his books and wanted to meet him so I called him up. He invited me to visit. I arrived at his home in La Jolla, California, up on a hillside overlooking a long stretch of surf and beach. I rang the bell and he opened the door to greet me. He was wearing only a red bathing suit. It was summer but not hot. I felt a little overdressed in my suit and tie but that didn't bother Rogers at all. He had me sit on a comfortable sofa and he took an armchair beside a table. I thanked him for permitting the visit and we exchanged pleasantries. After a bit I began talking about difficulties teachers had in implementing student choice in learning, which Rogers advocated. In the middle of a sentence the phone at Dr. Rogers's elbow began to ring. I stopped talking so he could answer it. Rogers never flinched. You would have thought him deaf. He nodded to me and said, "Yes, go on." He listened intently to what I was saying, right through the noise of the phone. I had never seen anybody do that. I've noticed that people even when engaged in the most interesting conversation will jump up and answer the phone when it rings. They feel obliged to. Never mind that it might be a wrong number or a sales pitch. We can't resist answering so we abandon the person at hand. I learned from Carl Rogers that when you are speaking with someone you should make them the prime focus of your attention. He taught me that telephones can be disregarded, which came as a revelation. After that day, I followed his example with telephones and impressed a few people by it. A few years after my meeting with Rogers, telephone answering machines came into vogue and since then I've let them do the answering for me.

Thomas Gordon, author of the acclaimed *Parent Effectiveness Training* (1970), *Teacher Effectiveness Training* (1974), and *Discipline That Works* (1989), has made major contributions to effective listening. Like Rogers, Gordon believes people work out their problems best by talking them through. The process goes better when a skilled listener draws people out and helps them clarify their concerns. Gordon devised a set of listening skills to help parents and teachers do this. He called the skills passive listening, acknowledgment, door openers, and active listening. Suppose you are listening to Julian who is trying to explain why yet again he has not completed his homework. As Julian begins to speak, you use *passive listening*. You say nothing, but show receptiveness by eye contact, taking a seat by Julian, and remaining alert. When Julian begins to talk you show attentiveness through *acknowledgment responses* such as nodding and saying "uh-huh" and "I see." If he has difficulty saying what's on his mind, you may use *door openers* to help him get started, such as, "Could you tell me more?" or "It sounds like you have something to say about that." As Julian expresses himself you use *active listening* in which you show understanding of his message by reflecting it back. Without making judgments, you say something like, "You are not able to get your homework done because your mother makes you work after school and then mind your little brother while she works at night."

Though Gordon's listening techniques are widely used, they have been criticized for limiting the listener's ability to understand the speaker deeply. Stephen R. Covey (1989) contends that when we use active listening we do injustice to those speaking because the process is likely to turn their thinking toward our view of reality and away from theirs. To listen properly, Covey says, is to focus our powers on understanding what the student is saying *within the student's perception of reality*. He calls this process **empathetic listening,** which he says helps us gain a much better understanding of the other person.

Understanding

When I visited Carl Rogers he gave me a second lesson that was actually more important than telephone ignoring, though less flashy—he demonstrated a level of listening I had rarely seen. He seemed to be doing what Covey says, to understand what I was saying from my point of view, not his. I didn't grasp that lesson until some time later when I finally realized that what you try to do is "get inside the heads" of students you are communicating with. You make yourself aware not just of their words, but of their deeper hopes, fears, realities, and difficulties. The way to do this is to listen *within* the student's frame of reference as child or adolescent rather than from your frame of reference as adult teacher. What the student considers reality usually differs, sometimes remarkably, from what we consider reality. If we are to know and work well with students, we need to know not just their thoughts but what those thoughts mean in their personal existence.

One of the habits of highly successful people, Covey says, is gaining understanding of others before trying to make them understand you. He writes:

> If I were to summarize in one sentence the single most important
> principle I have learned in the field of interpersonal relations, it

would be this: *Seek first to understand, then to be understood.*
This principle is the key to effective interpersonal communication. (1989, p. 237)

Most of us, Covey suggests, do not know how to listen empathetically and thus may not properly understand the other person. When others talk to us we may only pretend to listen (as when someone chatters on and we occasionally reply, "yeah" and "uh-huh"). At times we may listen selectively, catching only what we want to hear while letting the rest slip past. Or we may actually do our best to listen attentively by paying close attention to the words being said. But even with attentive listening we are unlikely to gain real understanding unless we can gain some entry into the other person's reality. We can't actually walk a mile in their shoes, but we must try to see what it would be like to do so. Covey reminds us:

Empathetic listening takes time, but it doesn't take anywhere near as much time as it takes to back up and correct misunderstandings when you're already miles down the road, to redo, to live with unexpressed and unsolved problems . . . People want to be understood. And whatever investment of time it takes to do that will bring much greater returns of time as you work from an accurate understanding of (their) problems and issues. . . . (1989, p. 253)

Reacting Helpfully

When it was time for the math lesson, Monique said to Mrs. Adello, "I don't feel good. Can I just lay my head down on the desk?"

Jordan, when asked for his trigonometry homework, said to Mr. Sánchez, "I don't see the point of this stuff. What does it have to do with anything in real life?"

Susan tells Ms. Sparks, her physical education teacher, "In my old school we didn't do these exercises. We played games or did some other kinds of activities that were like really really fun instead of this exercise stuff which I know is good for you I guess but I mean why do it? It's just like, well you know, who wants it?"

What are these students telling their teachers? Are the messages what they appear or do they imply more than the words indicate? Usually when speaking to the teacher students simply answer questions or ask for help. At times, however, they may be giving us significant messages. Monique may tell you she doesn't feel well and mean literally that. Or it could be that her real message is something else. "I don't feel well" might actually mean "I'll do almost anything, including lying, to get out of this lesson."

When we understand underlying messages, opportunities open for improving instruction and enhancing relationships. When you think you might be hearing such a message, listen to the tone of voice and observe body mannerisms. They may tell you a great deal about the student's needs and how that student is reacting to you. Students hardly ever express their needs directly. They won't tell you, "I really need more attention from you." or "I don't feel like I'm accepted by the class—what can you do to help me?" But they often indicate those things, sometimes through body language, even when their words say something different. See if you agree with the analyses that follow each of the following cases. (The true meaning may be literal or may underlie the words or actions. Please understand that the analyses are just one possible view of reality and that the suggested responses provide a good chance of success but are not infallible. If the responses don't seem appropriate to you, use your understanding, creativity, and tact to come up with more suitable ones.)

1. Early in the geometry lesson, John, holding his brow, says to Miss Stapleton, "I don't feel good. Can I go to the nurse's station?"
   Analysis: John may actually be ill or he may be trying to get out of the lesson. Here you'd best let him go to the nurse's station where he can rest or receive medical attention if needed. If this pattern repeats, find a quiet opportunity to talk with him. "John, I am wondering if there is something about the class that is making you feel upset. If there is, I'd like to know. I want the class to be good for everyone and that includes you. I'd really appreciate your help."

2. Miss Stapleton, circulating among working students, sees Maree has made no progress. She asks why and Maree says, "This is too hard. I don't understand it."
   Analysis: The work may actually be too hard for Maree, as she says, or her mind may be entirely elsewhere. If you believe she is troubled by a personal problem, say, "I'm sorry, Maree, I hadn't realized you were not understanding. I truly want you to enjoy this work. Do you just not feel like doing the work right now? What could I do to help?" These words may not resolve Maree's difficulty, but they will give her attention and comfort.

3. When Miss Stapleton collects homework, she finds Miguel hasn't done his. She says in front of the class, "Miguel, you had the assignment just like everybody else. I don't want any excuses. You haven't tried." Miguel replies, "You know why? That stuff is stupid. Nobody goes around bisecting lines with a compass. That's the dumbest thing I ever heard of."
   Analysis: Miss Stapleton has made two mistakes. The first is in not learning enough about Miguel to foresee his reaction and the second is reprimanding Miguel in front of the class. If you make this mistake, get out of the situation with the least possible damage to Miguel's dignity and your own. About the best you can do is say, also before the class, "Miguel, I can see you don't feel good about this work. I may have made a mistake in judgment. I want to make the class worthwhile for everyone. Perhaps we can discuss how to do that, as a class. Could I ask

for your cooperation, Miguel? Let's think about it overnight and discuss it tomorrow." Miguel will not decline your request. He may be the only student reacting negatively, but what you have said lets him off the hook and gives you a reprieve as well.

4. When Mr. Sellars tells his fourth-grade students to take out their spelling books, he hears a chorus of groans.

    Analysis: The groans deliver a sincere message. You know that when students are bored in school it is not their fault, and you know the futility of reprimanding or lecturing them about the value of spelling. So you say, "Class, I can see you don't enjoy this activity. I think good spelling is very important and I hope you think so, too. Maybe we can find a better way to learn our spelling words. Would you think about it overnight? Tomorrow, let's discuss what you have thought about and see if we can make things better. For right now, let's try making a story using the words. Jason, give me a sentence that includes the first word on the list. I'll write what you say on the board. You make sure I spell the words correctly."

5. Mr. Sellars checks each student's progress on their practice sheet. He finds Amy has done nothing at all. He stands looking at her. She begins to chew her nail.

    Analysis: Mr. Sellars has made mistakes in his lessons that you will avoid. You will know better than to give assignments that students might not work on. You will have established trust with Amy that makes her want to cooperate with you. If she is having trouble, you ask, "Amy, would you like to work with Kristin on this assignment? Let's see what the two of you together can do."

6. Kindergarten teacher Ms. Terrero tells Allen to put down the toy and go sit in the circle. He says, "No," and looks at her and laughs.

    Analysis: Kindergarten children do not respond to reason as older children do. You quietly say, "We can't wait for you, Allen. I'll hold the toy for you so you can have it back later. Come now and sit by me. It's time for our story and I need you to help." You take his hand and lead him to the circle. Because Allen wants your attention he goes willingly.

7. Ms. Terrero is trying to teach students to raise their hands before speaking. Delores speaks to Ms. Terrero every minute or so without raising her hand. She tugs at Ms. Terrero's skirt several times a day.

    Analysis: You judge that Delores feels insecure, not yet adjusted to being separated from her mother. You pat her, smile at her, and chat with her in a friendly manner. When she speaks out in class you ignore her and say, "I'm looking for someone who remembers to raise their hand." Soon Delores raises her hand. When she does you call on her and thank her for remembering.

Emotions and Underlying Messages

When you detect underlying messages, you find emotion. Emotion relates to needs. Students need to feel secure, feel they belong, believe they have a good chance of success, receive attention, have fun, feel competent, and maintain their sense of personal dignity. When they feel insecure, they make their worries known in one way or another. When they don't feel part of the group, they withdraw or act out. When they need attention they may clamor for it, often in undesirable ways. When they find no pleasure in assignments you give them, they go through the motions reluctantly. When they do not feel accepted, they may overcompensate by showing off or defying you. Students avoid at all costs situations that threaten their personal dignity. They fear looking stupid or inept, so they show indifference. They detest being backed into a corner and often lash back when they are. Look back at the cases and see if you detect emotion in what the students say.

Encouraging

Some of the responses made in these hypothetical examples illustrate what Haim Ginott called **congruent communication**, which he defined as communication that is harmonious with students' feelings about situations and themselves. This type of communication provides encouragement. It corrects undesirable behavior but does not put students down. Teachers don't say, "You are very inconsiderate about the noise you are causing." or "Well, I see you've made another mess." Such comments cause bad feelings and do not encourage students to use better judgment. You must remember conscientiously to avoid comments that:

- Label students by referring to them as lazy, thoughtless, inconsiderate, bad helper, poor citizen, and so on.
- Ask rhetorical "why" questions (Why did you write this so poorly? Why are you two talking? Why do I have to tell you this again?)
- Give moralistic lectures. (You are not making an effort to get along with each other. You will never get anywhere in life if you can't get along with other people.
- Make caustic or sarcastic remarks to students. (I simply don't believe that; you're not telling the truth. Oh yes, how odd; that's the fourth time you've lost your assignment.)
- Deny students' feelings. (You have no reason to cry. There is absolutely nothing to worry about.)
- Demand students' cooperation. (That's enough fooling around. Get back in your seats and get to work.)
- Lose your temper and self-control. (How dare you speak to me in that manner! I am the teacher in this room and you darned well better remember it!)

When students are worried or have made a mistake, our objective is to help them. Yet when trying to be helpful we often push them away. Thomas Gordon (*T.E.T.: Teacher Effectiveness Training, 1974*) has listed 12 common types of teacher responses that stifle communication. He calls them **roadblocks to communication**. A few examples are given here. To see what Gordon means, imagine that student Dale is supposed to be writing a composition in class. Dale learned just last night his parents intend to separate. He didn't sleep much and now can't concentrate on the assignment. Dale could use some comfort and kindness, but Mr. Askew does not detect his need. Mr. Askew thinks Dale is procrastinating, which he sometimes does. Mr. Askew asks Dale what the problem is. Dale shrugs and says "Nothing." Then he adds that he doesn't understand how to do the assignment. The following are examples of comments Mr. Askew might then make that would discourage Dale and make him unwilling to talk further.

Giving orders "Dale, you get busy. I think you know how to do that composition. No more wasting time. Get your name and date on your paper and get to work."

Warning "Dale, I'm telling you for the last time to get to work. If you don't, you'll be taking that home with you tonight along with a note to your parents."

Preaching "Dale, you know you are expected to complete all your work. We are not doing this for the fun of it. It's for your own good, don't you see that? If you don't try to learn this, you're never going to write well at all. You will never look like an educated person."

Advising Mr. Askew says, "Dale, let me give you a piece of advice. When I was younger I was much like you, never doing what I was capable of. A good teacher got me out of that. He told me to set some personal goals for myself and work toward them, step by step. I think you'd benefit from that. I'd like you to come up with a plan and try it."

Criticizing "Dale, I can't believe you are fooling around again. Didn't we just talk about this last week? You have ability but you are not using it. I'm really disappointed in you." (Dale says nothing.)

Questioning "What's wrong, Dale? You have been sitting here ten minutes and still have nothing on that paper. You aren't even trying. Do you think something bad is going to happen if you write a few lines? What's the matter with you anyhow?"

While Mr. Askew's responses to Dale may be common, they do not help. Instead they make Dale feel worse. Each time this happens, Dale becomes less inclined to approach Mr. Askew for help. What should Mr. Askew have said to Dale? Consider the following responses which instead of finding fault with Dale provide encouragement:

- "Dale, we need to get this assignment completed by the end of the period."
- "Writing is not easy, is it? Many people have a difficult time at first. Let's see if we can begin with a title. What would your composition be about?"

- "Sometimes we feel like working and sometimes we don't. We might be tired or our minds might be elsewhere. Do you ever have feelings like that?"
- "Dale, I can tell you are having difficulty getting started. Is there something about the assignment that bothers you? I'd like to correct it, if there is."
- "Dale, I feel something is not right for you. I don't want to pry. If you feel like talking, I'll listen now or I'll be here in this room right after school."

Teachers set up communication roadblocks regularly. They are trying to be helpful but don't realize what they say has the opposite effect. Even with "better" responses from Mr. Askew, Dale might choose to keep his troubles to himself. But he will at least talk with Mr. Askew, which will be better for both of them than struggling against each other.

To encourage students to cooperate, we should acknowledge the validity of their feelings. We accomplish nothing positive by denying their feelings or trying to make them comply. That degrades their dignity and makes things worse. We should always keep foremost in mind what Ginott called the teachers' **hidden asset**: He says we should always ask ourselves the following:

HOW CAN I BE MOST HELPFUL TO MY STUDENTS RIGHT NOW?

If they are violating a class agreement, we help them by addressing the situation and inviting them to cooperate. If their behavior is improper, we calmly repeat directions or expectations. If they lose self control, we give them a good example by remaining calm and asking how we can help.

WHY YOU SHOULDN'T ARGUE WITH STUDENTS

Many teachers, when students complain about assignments, make excuses, or claim the teacher is wrong, slip out of the helpful mode into the confrontive mode. They don't want to listen to what they feel is untrue and don't want to accept bogus explanations students use to get off the hook. Most of all, they don't like to be told they are wrong. Their natural inclination, like that of anyone, is to dispute the contention and argue. However, that is one of the worst traps teachers can fall into. They defeat themselves every time, for two reasons: They never win the argument, and in trying to win they damage student trust.

Gerry Spence wrote a best-selling book claiming you can argue and win every time, but what Spence meant by "win" is for both parties to get very nearly what they want. We are not speaking of that kind of arguing, but of the kind where one person tries to convince the other by means of reasoning (or often a louder voice). When teachers argue this way, they cannot win. Even with superior intellect and impeccable reasoning they seldom bring students to their point of view. Why? To argue is to challenge the other person, which makes them put up defenses and gird their loins for battle. Virtually always, both teacher and student end up more firmly convinced than ever they are right. Meanwhile, both have had their feelings battered and thereafter don't much care for each other's company. As Dale Carnegie (1981, p. 116) said:

> There is only one way under high heaven to get the best of an argument—and that is to avoid it. Avoid it as you would avoid rattlesnakes and earthquakes.

What then should you do when disagreements with students arise? The best thing is to honestly consider their point of view. Perhaps you are wrong; if so, you should admit it and go on from there. Perhaps a middle ground can be reached that satisfies both of you. Here is how to proceed:

- Listen carefully to the student. Keep calm. Hear them out. Don't deny or contradict what they say.
- Drop your defenses. If you are offended, resist the impulse to strike back. Try for understanding.
- Don't tell the student he or she is wrong. Doing so hits at their intelligence, perception, and reason—in other words, at their personal dignity.
- When students have had their say, tell them you have considered carefully what they said. Say, "I am often wrong, but. . . ." Then briefly state your position. Tell them you'd like to find a solution to the disagreement that satisfies their concerns as well as yours. If that can't be done immediately, set the issue aside temporarily and discuss it further when feelings have subsided.

This is not to say you should never try to change students' opinions. One of your main duties is to help them see different points of view and allow them to change their behavior when doing so will serve them better. But you don't accomplish this broadening of view by arguing with students. You accomplish it through example, stories, lessons, and class discussion. And, of course, you can give your own opinion as well. Ben Franklin is supposed to have said:

> If you argue and rankle and contradict, you may achieve a victory sometimes; but it will be an empty victory because you will never get your opponent's goodwill.

Presumably Franklin knew what he was talking about. He was instrumental in bringing men of iron will and greatly diverse views into agreements that emerged as the United States Constitution, one of the greatest documents in human history.

STRUCTURES FOR COMMUNICATION

Most communication between teachers and students occurs as ongoing chat, instructional input, questions about assignments, and discussions about lessons and other issues. This communication is *nonstructured*. It happens sporadically and flows through normal interactions and teaching. In these interactions you always display your ethics and when possible contribute to student dignity. In addition to this nonstructured communication, you will find it helpful to organize times when communication is done for reasons other than instruction. We will call this communication *structured* because it is done for specific purposes and in specific ways. Four types of structured communication are especially useful: (1) giving students personal attention, (2) reviewing feelings about learning, (3) discussing class business and concerns, and (4) informing parents about class activities and progress. Let's see briefly how each can be done and what it accomplishes.

Giving Students Personal Attention

Each student wants to be validated by the teacher, to feel noticed and valued. Students who receive regular attention feel better and don't act out as much. Some teachers give personal attention as students enter the room. They smile, say hello, and greet as many as possible by name. Primary teachers sometimes touch each student on the head. Some teachers, while circulating among students at work, stop by each student and quietly ask a question or make a positive comment. If you can't get around to every student every day, make sure to distribute your attention evenly.

Reviewing Feelings about Learning

Teachers routinely have students review their progress but usually focus on what students have learned rather than on the activities they have enjoyed. Students' reactions to instruction can teach you more than any textbook. If you are an elementary teacher, you should set aside a few minutes at the end of each day for students to discuss what they liked best and least in the activities you provided. If you are a secondary teacher, you should set aside 15 minutes a couple of times a week for similar reviews. Drop your defenses and let students speak frankly. Ultimately you will be grateful for what they teach you.

Discussing Class Business and Concerns

Teachers everywhere use class meetings for students to express concerns about the class and solve group problems. Class meetings were popularized by William Glasser in his 1969 book *Schools Without Failure*, one of the century's most influential books in education. Glasser felt communication about group concerns occurred best when the class is seated in a tight circle so everyone can have eye contact. The teacher serves as leader to get the discussion under way, then acts as a group member. The operating principle of class meetings is that problems are identified and solutions sought, but blame is never assigned. Everyone has their say. Any student or the teacher can raise concerns. The group seeks a solution acceptable to all. The teacher makes sure that each student is heard and no one is ridiculed or blamed.

Many authorities on discipline and instruction advocate class meetings. How does one introduce them? Jane Nelsen, Lynn Lott, and H. Stephen Glenn (1997) advise telling students you would like them to consider holding meetings where they can help make decisions about the class. Middle school and high school students may need persuading. Using language appropriate for your grade level, initiate a discussion about power and how it is so often used to resolve problems in school. Discuss how in power methods teachers tell kids what to do. The kids then comply or rebel, without being brought into the decision. To encourage discussion, Nelsen, Lott, and Glenn (p. 33) suggest asking students:

> Who has an example they would like to share about what happens when someone tries to control you? What do you feel? What do you do? What do you learn? How do you try to control or manipulate others, including teachers?

Kids will usually say that power methods make them feel angry or scared and manipulated. They understand power methods give them only two options, to comply or else rebel and suffer the consequences.

Ask them if they would like to be more involved in the decisions that affect their lives. Point out that some students actually prefer having adults boss them around, so they can rebel or so they won't have to take responsibility for themselves. This kind of discussion is especially helpful and effective in classrooms where students have been taught with authoritarian methods. Once students show willingness to try class meetings, suggest times when they might be held. Have frequent meetings while students are learning the process. After that, a half-hour meeting per week will usually suffice.

Informing Parents about Class Activities and Progress

Teachers acquire reputations in interesting ways. Usually they are considered to be good teachers if parents like them, average if parents don't know anything about them, and not so good if parents dislike them. Parents form their impressions from how you treat their child and how well you keep them informed of their child's progress. Most parents think you're neat if you treat their kid well but get very upset if they think you don't. Because your sense of well-being, not to mention parental support, is affected by how parents see you, it is worth keeping them informed about your program and their child. You can do this occasionally by telephone, but a concise class newsletter works better. In it, tell what the class has been doing and what future plans are. Mention every student by name if possible. Give the newsletter a professional appearance. From third grade on, students can do the write-ups. You can edit and organize the newsletter and print it. Students can deliver it home. This doesn't take much time. Students enjoy the process and results, and so do parents. It does wonders for your reputation.

WHERE DO WE GO FROM HERE?

We have completed consideration of four of the nine elements that play predominant roles in class synergy: ethics, trust, charisma, and communication. Five remain to be explored. The next element, the topic of Chapter 5, is one we've already mentioned repeatedly—making lessons interesting.

TO THINK ABOUT

1. Many teachers believe it is not what you say to students that matters, but how you treat them. Others maintain you can do or say anything to students so long as you command their respect. Do you agree or disagree with these views? How would you explain your point of view to another?

2. Haim Ginott said that discipline is not something you achieve immediately through discipline techniques but rather a series of little victories in which you gradually win students over. What do you think of that notion? Do you feel Ginott's advice on how to speak with students is really all that important? If students make you angry or disgusted, is it wrong for you to react in accordance with your true feelings?

3. Thomas Gordon's roadblocks to communication are actually things most teachers have said to students for decades—questioning them about their motives, giving them advice, moralizing, analyzing their actions, and giving them warnings. Are these not time-honored responses we all expect of teachers? Gordon even lists praise as a roadblock. How could giving praise and advice work against communication?

4. Suppose you decided to produce a class newsletter for parents. What would you want to include? What would you like the appearance to be? Should you let students decide? What if you don't like their decision?

5

LET'S MAKE SCHOOL INTERESTING FOR STUDENTS

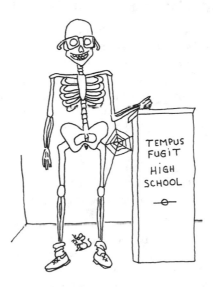

Mr. Stanke had determined to wait until students wanted to do things his way.

MY DEAR MISS OSBORNE

I had some great teachers in my young days, but none made school more interesting than Miss Osborne did. That was fifth grade so it was a long time ago, yet some of the experiences are as vivid as yesterday. When we were learning about the early colonists, we made and wore paper costumes. We acted out John Alden's pursuit of Priscilla Mullins on behalf of Miles Standish and heard Priscilla (Joyce Black) ask John (me) why he didn't speak for himself. We parched corn, smashed it into meal, made cornbread, and ate it with butter. We carded wool and used a spinning wheel to spin it into thread. At another time we learned Latin American dances, especially the rumba, and put on a dance performance for the school. We had some spelling and math competitions against the other fifth grade. There was so much activity we often had a parent or two in the room helping out. There were quiet times, too. Miss Osborne read to us every day—my favorite book was *Pinocchio*. I don't remember our misbehaving much. Maybe we did and I've forgotten, but I don't think so. I contrast that year with my sixth-grade year in the same school. I can only remember two things that happened in sixth grade. The teacher let us sing rounds of "Row Row Row Your Boat", which I liked, and she gave me a grade of zero on a spelling test because, though I had spelled every word correctly I had, for some reason, put a dot above every letter. In the teacher's view that made all the words incorrect. Or maybe she just wanted to teach me a lesson.

CURRICULUM: THE IDEAL AND THE REAL

There have been at least a hundred books written about curriculum—what school should offer students and how it should be organized. At least two hundred books have been written about instruction—how teachers should deliver the curriculum. There have been hundreds of thousands of university lectures on curriculum and instruction, telling what has been, is, should be, shouldn't have been, and how you ought to do it. If you boiled all of those books and lectures down to two drops, you would have:

1. The curriculum should provide knowledge and skills that benefit students and society.
2. Instruction should be interesting and effective.

Those two principles give all the guidelines needed for quality education. Teachers supply the details. They set the learning table with food for the mind. But something goes wrong in many classrooms. Some students will barely nibble at the macaroni we serve them. Most swallow it; some like it. Some push it away. Some get up and leave the table.

What goes here? Nothing really mysterious. Steve Biddulph, in his great book entitled *Raising Boys*, puts it well:

> The learning environment of today's schools seems designed to educate senior citizens, not young people at their most energetic. Everyone is supposed to be quiet, nice, and compliant. Excitement doesn't seem to belong in this kind of learning (though many wonderful teachers do manage to bring some fun and energy into their classes, and many children catch this spirit and run with it). The passivity required by school contradicts everything we know about kids, especially adolescents. Adolescence is the age of passion. Boys and girls crave an engaged and intense learning experience, with men and women who challenge them and get to know them personally—and from this specific knowledge of their needs, work with them to shape and extend their intellect, spirit, and skills. If kids aren't waking up in the morning saying, 'Wow! School today!' then something is not right. (1997, p. 130)

I don't necessarily agree that something is wrong when kids don't jump out of bed and exclaim, "Wow! School today!" That's not much in keeping with what I've seen in teenagers. And certainly many students like school. But I agree with Biddulph, in the main. Children of all ages have a passion for learning, but their passion seldom takes the direction we'd like. Lots of them would rather spend days in the video arcade than in school. We dismiss them as wayward truants and losers. But we can't brush off the bright students who say they learn more and have a better time facing the computer monitor than they do in school. That ought to tell us something is out of kilter in education.

Biddulph maintains that the young, especially adolescents, have a surplus of passion and talent that enables them to do things of real significance—a goal they have trouble reaching at the arcade. With opportunity and direction they would involve themselves in something real, creative, perhaps socially useful. When they don't have that opportunity, their energy finds its way into misbehavior and trouble-making. Not to sound like a broken record, but . . .

- Students like activities that are fun, interesting, and challenging.
- They detest activities that are boring.
- When bored too long, they find something interesting to do, usually something we don't approve of.

We have known this since the dawn of history, or at least for several centuries. But you wouldn't think so.

How to Make School Interesting and Worthwhile

Let's acknowledge that a great percentage of students don't like school. Let's not argue about whether what we provide there is good for them. Let's think instead about how to make school good for students *and* have them like it too. Let's explore a strategy that will lure most students and keep them in class willingly. It consists of five parts. Some of the information you need is presented in the paragraphs that follow. You can add additional information by observing and talking with your students. Once that is done, you can accomplish all five parts, which are:

1. Understand what your students are like—what they are capable of, incapable of, interested in, and predisposed to do.
2. Identify your students' needs and preferences and adapt instruction to them.
3. Let students help select topics and activities that interest them.
4. Spice up topics that are not naturally interesting, or persuasively explain to your students how the topics benefit them.
5. When appropriate, consider using a facilitative style of teaching.

Let's see what these five parts entail.

1. Understand What Your Students Are Like   The following sections describe students generally at different stages of development. If you like, you can read all of them and get a picture of how students change over time. Or if you prefer, feel free, in the spirit of escaping boredom, to give attention only to the age level that interests you.

PRIMARY GRADES (AGES 5 TO 8)   Children first come to school full of life and eager to learn. Most have a loving disposition. They are receptive to most everything you introduce. They especially enjoy stories, music, and rhythmic activities. Many, especially the girls whose language develops quickly, give the impression of being intellectually precocious. Their intellect is not what it appears, however. Until approximately age seven they function at what Swiss psychologist Jean Piaget called the preoperational stage, where they are unable to do logical reasoning. (See Jean Piaget, 1951, or C. M. Charles, 1974.) Until that time they are poor at remembering the order of events, understanding rules, explaining relationships, comprehending numbers and number relationships, and understanding other speakers accurately, including the teacher. They get along reasonably well with others, though they squabble a lot. They tire easily and get fussy, so require frequent rest. They make little distinction between work and play. At around age seven they begin to mature noticeably. Intellectually, they become able to consider the relationship of parts to whole and are thus able to reason logically. Where previously they reasoned and explained on the basis of appearances or intuition (e.g., The sun moves because the wind blows it along), they can now understand number relationships and science concepts such as why we have day and night. They are learning to play well together. By second grade they are enjoying games such as tag and hide-and-seek. They like puzzles, riddles, and guessing games. Although they can learn rules for games, they are poor at following them. They accept adult authority with little question. They lie routinely but should not be considered dishonest—they are not completely able to separate fact from fiction. They are highly imitative of each other. For them, misbehavior is whatever adults don't like, and guilt is getting caught. Before leaving the primary level they have become socialized to raising hands, standing in lines, taking turns, and waiting patiently. They continue to respond well to affection and personal attention.

INTERMEDIATE GRADES(AGES 9 TO 11)   As students move into the fourth grade, they become increasingly independent, though they still want attention and affection from teachers. Holding hands with the teacher takes the place of hugging. Intellectually, their ability to think logically grows stronger. They use concrete language for thinking—they cannot yet think in terms of pure abstractions. Socially, they have become highly argumentative. Many are loud and abusive, yet there is increasing evidence of reason and persuasion. They like to play group games and show an increasing bent for competition. Losing is difficult to accept; many cry and throw temper tantrums. They recognize the need for rules and rule enforcement, both in games and class behavior. No longer is teacher authority blindly accepted. Students may argue with teachers, talk back, and drag their heels. They show a growing awareness of honesty and its importance in relationships. They see that the more a lie intends to deceive, the worse it is. Conscience develops along with respect for others. A growing sense of right and wrong is evident. While still obedient to teachers, children at this age no longer consider adults infallible. They are growing in respect for each other and increasingly want to share each others' company. They like group names and begin to form gangs, clubs, and cliques. Their behavior begins to reflect peer norms.

MIDDLE SCHOOL GRADES (AGES 12 TO 14) Behavior suddenly becomes much more diverse among students at the middle school level, and teachers must have exceptional skill in order to teach well and build supportive relationships. Bodily changes worry, perplex, excite, and dismay these students. New realities of an opposite sex stir and baffle. Psychological weaning from parents leaves them feeling lost and cut off. They crave adult support, yet the emerging need for independence produces conflict with adults. If that were not enough, they are required to adjust to new school organization, curriculum, and styles of teaching. These factors provide serious distractions to learning. Meanwhile, students are becoming increasingly rebellious and disposed to probing at outer limits of rules and customs. Their awe of the teacher has waned, but is replaced with respect and affection for those who show understanding and helpfulness. Intellectually, these students have acquired an awesome new power—the ability to think abstractly. Their intellect is as efficient as that of adults though they don't yet have adult wisdom. They can make use of concepts such as love, hate, honesty, loyalty, negative number, force, speed, time, and atomic particles. They have become able to think about thought.

HIGH SCHOOL GRADES (AGES 15 TO 18)   Before entering high school, students have become able to do deep thinking. They now show a proclivity for theorizing. Everything has a cause, a purpose, a place. They think about the possible as much as the actual and have acquired a strong sense of right and wrong. Their rational power produces the idealism characteristic of adolescence. Propositional thinking emerges: If I do so and so, then so and so will result. Interest in nature and society balloons to the extent that many, in their awe, begin to feel inadequate, incapable of dealing with the universe and society around them. A lie is now seen as anything intentionally false. Breaking rules and laws is no longer seen as absolutely wrong. Punishment must take into account factors such as intent to break a law, age of the violator, and previous record of behavior. Many rules and laws are seen as wrong, so there is no harm in breaking them. Socially, these students can see various groups' points of view, which they like to weigh, clarify, and evaluate against each other. They can't see why everything is not ideal—ideal politics, institutions, human relations, and so forth—which makes them overly critical of the way institutions and people actually function. Students may scathingly reject existing social arrangements and values. Their behavior, however, usually indicates adherence to existing social norms. As they near the end of high school, students begin to settle down emotionally. They understand themselves better and have reached a truce with their bodies and feelings. They have begun to think about what they hope to do in the future. Some, lamentably, become further alienated from the educational mainstream. A new relationship with adults emerges. The love–hate attitude of earlier years fades, while respect for adults grows as students recognize their own interdependence with the community. Teachers can now treat these students as fellow adults, granting them wide power in making decisions about their own learning. Students see teachers as guides and role models.

2. Identify Your Students' Needs and Preferences and Adapt Instruction to Them   In recent decades, teaching has become progressively more difficult. This is due to changing attitudes among the young about adult authority and the value of school. Some years ago, psychiatrist William Glasser (1990) described teaching as the hardest job in the world. He expressed sympathy for teachers, especially those at the middle school and secondary levels. He found that they yearned to work with dedicated, high-achieving students, but were continually frustrated because so few of their students made an effort to learn.

Glasser said the hundreds of teachers with whom he had talked reported their main discipline problems were not disruption or defiance, but overwhelming apathy. They couldn't get students to try. Students would participate only half-heartedly in class activities and wouldn't do homework at all. Glasser talked to those students, too, and they reported that their reluctance was not because schoolwork was too hard, but because it was too boring. Students and teachers are caught in adjoining traps. Students won't try because they are bored and don't see any value in what they are asked to learn. Teachers try to make them learn but in doing so only make things worse. As teachers threaten and punish, they further alienate the very people they are trying to help. That leaves everybody frustrated, with little hope of things getting better.

Yet the way out of the trap is right before our eyes. It lies in making school interesting and worthwhile. At present, school is not doing a good job of meeting students' needs. If it were, students would find it rewarding and teachers' lives would be much easier.

STUDENTS' NEEDS   What are students' needs? In relation to school and classroom, they are the following:

1. Security
2. Hope
3. Acceptance

4. Dignity
5. Power
6. Enjoyment
7. Competence

These needs are distinct from interests, preferences, or "wants." A need is something a person craves permanently. Take acceptance, for example. When we don't feel accepted in school, we feel insignificant and anchorless. We will go to lengths to get somebody to think highly of us. If we don't get it from the teacher we will try to get it from peers, even if it means doing something that gets us in trouble.

An interest or a want, in contrast, relates to something we would like to have, but its absence does not trouble us unduly and the desire is transient. For example, you may want to go to a particular movie. Your desire to go may be very strong, but you don't lose sleep over it. If you don't get to go, you forget all about it after a time. Let's examine this list of needs a bit further.

1. *Security* We all want to feel comfortable wherever we go and especially want to avoid the anxiety that comes from fear of threat and intimidation. If students are to be successful in school, they must feel secure in the classroom and school. They cannot learn very much when continually worried about being outcasts or fearing intimidation. For the most part, schools do a good job meeting students' need for security, but a surprising number of students say they are worried every day about being bullied or intimidated.

2. *Hope* Hope is the expectation that things will get better in the future, or at least won't get worse. It keeps us going, and looking forward. We all crave it and are badly affected when we lose it. Students in school hope they will be successful. They hope they will learn things of importance and have a nice time doing so and nobody will mistreat them. The students Glasser wrote of, those who have quit trying, are students who have lost hope. They no longer think there's a reasonable chance of getting anything worthwhile out of school.

3. *Acceptance* All of us need to feel accepted, to believe we have an acknowledged and important place in the family, school, class, and other groups. That applies just as much to children as it does to you and me. We feel accepted when others acknowledge us, give us attention, appreciate our efforts, and recognize our achievements. School helps many students feel accepted, but unfortunately some students experience so little acceptance they continually act out in an effort to acquire it.

4. *Dignity* Dignity refers to self-image. The need for a strong positive self-image emerges in early childhood and reaches its peak in adolescence. Students want to feel competent. They want to project an image as intelligent, capable, "cool," adept,

strong, and loyal. They will fight, sometimes tooth and nail, to protect their self-image. Self-protection is the reason behind defensiveness, unwillingness to try, withdrawal, and counter attack. School can build self-image but can also threaten it.

5. *Power*   All of us want to feel we have some control over our lives and events in which we are involved. This need emerges before we can talk and continues through life. We want to make decisions for ourselves, even if they are wrong, rather than always have somebody tell us what to do. School mostly directs students; it doesn't give them many opportunities to make decisions that affect them and the group.

6. *Enjoyment*   Students continually look for enjoyment, though what constitutes enjoyment varies from situation to situation and person to person. For the most part, this need is satisfied by teacher charisma, interaction with fellow students, group competition, challenge, collaboration, exploring personal interests, and working at tasks considered worthwhile. Though we have known this for a long time, we still do an inadequate job of providing enjoyment in school.

7. *Competence*   Every student wants to know a great deal, not only know information but understand it. All students would like to be highly skilled in something. School has unique potential for helping students meet this need, but something gets in the way. We blame boredom, disinterest, and sometimes poor relations with the teacher. However, the main reason school doesn't make most students truly competent is that we don't help students learn what truly interests them.

STUDENT LEARNING PREFERENCES   Students learn and enjoy school more when encouraged to work in ways they prefer. Students do not like to learn as teachers usually want them to. There are exceptions of course, but in general they don't like, for long, to sit still, keep quiet, or work by themselves. They don't like to memorize facts and regurgitate them on tests. They don't like lengthy writing assignments. They don't like to do repetitive work. They don't like long reading assignments though many spend hours reading material that interests them. Most do not like individual competition where the same two or three students win all the time.

They do like to talk, work together, move about, do productive and creative work with their hands, and work on projects. They like variety. They enjoy team competition and trying to surpass their previous levels of achievement. They like to use computers and media. They like to hear and learn language that has rhythm, rhyme, and metaphor. They like to tell and listen to stories. They like to do role-playing, perform skits, and give performances for others. They like rhythmic activities with repetition, music, chanting, clapping, and dancing.

At the beginning of the chapter I mentioned my sixth-grade year in school and how little of it I can remember. I am sure my memory is blank because we did little besides listen to the teacher, read textbooks, memorize, and take tests. We never had activity as in Miss Osborne's room. That's not to say we can't learn through quiet introspective work, for we certainly can and do. But humans are more social than solitary, more active than phlegmatic, more verbal than reflective, and more physical than introspective. Our learning preferences reflect those traits.

3. Let Students Help Select Topics and Activities That Interest Them

Mr. Zellers teaches world history. He sets aside a portion of the course for current events and allows students to investigate in depth any they find particularly interesting. When a tidal wave killed thousands of people in Papua New Guinea in 1998, several of his students wanted to know more about tidal waves and why they are so devastating. Mr. Zellers allowed the students to decide how they would undertake the study and discussed resources they might find useful. As they got into the work, he helped them decide how much time they would require and what they would do or produce to indicate their learning. They decided they would like to make an illustrated presentation to other members of the class.

Just as students have preferred ways of learning, so do they have preferences about topics they wish to explore. Teachers fear if they allow student choice, the curriculum will degenerate into study of music stars and sports idols. Students are not that shallow. They will agree to pursue topics related to the curriculum. They don't object to worthwhile learnings. When you allow them options, have a number of possibilities at hand for them to consider. Even when students hate a required topic, they may have difficulty identifying something to take its place. If they don't like reading from textbooks about the parts of plants, suggest options such as bringing different plants to class to investigate how they are formed or growing beans or radishes in the room to see the parts develop. If they don't like studying and copying diagrams of the human body, ask what they might like to do instead. If they can't think of anything, suggest the possibility of using a model that can be taken apart and put back together or computer software that shows different layers of the body. Mr. Zellers, mentioned earlier, keeps close tabs on what is going on around the world and asks students to do the same. Together they review their lists of significant happenings. If students show strong interest in one of them he allows them to pursue it in more depth. At times students are investigating different topics. Usually they work in groups, but sometimes individually.

How does one initiate the practice of allowing student choice? Discuss the approach in class meetings. Explain to the students that you want to allow them some choice in topics so they can learn things they find especially interesting. Review the curriculum guide with them. Indicate what you feel must be covered, what you consider less essential, and what some possible options might be.

For several years William Glasser has been popularizing the concept of "quality teaching." He says today's education teaches fragments of information students remember just long enough to repeat on achievement tests. Most of that information has little value in their lives, he claims. Instead of that, Glasser would have teachers present only learnings students find enjoyable and useful. Everything else, he says, should be thrown out as nonsense. His criterion for what should be taught in school is this: **Students must clearly see the value in it.** Glasser says if students were allowed to select, they would choose mostly skill learning because they can see how skills help them in life. Knowledge would be taught only when it meets one of the following tests (Glasser, 1993):

1. The information is related to an important skill.
2. The information is something students express a desire to learn.
3. The information is something the teacher considers especially useful.
4. The information is required for college entrance exams.

Glasser's contentions are persuasive. However, we should think twice about tossing knowledge learning out with the bathwater. That would shortchange students. Being educated is more than being skillful. Education requires knowledge that puts us in touch with our universe, our society, our past, and our future. It shows us what is right and good, wrong and bad. Knowledge gives quality to life, even when it has no other practical value. It is not likely that most students will eagerly request the kinds of experience with art and music and literature that provide lifelong pleasure. They are not likely to ask for information about the universe, galaxies, atomic particles, and forces that make the universe work. I believe most of us have to be led into those things. One leads by charm, by example, by enthusiasm, by opening up possibilities, by asking provocative questions, by sharing aspects of life one is passionate about. We don't need to worry about making our horses drink. We only need to lead them to good water and let them see how much we enjoy it. They will follow.

4. Spice Up Topics That Are Not Naturally Interesting or Explain Their Benefits Even skills are not always interesting to students. Spelling is not a joyous undertaking for most. Neither is learning multiplication tables or the functions of sines, cosines, and tangents. Most students find studies of government stultifying. Yet, our lives are made better by knowing such things. How, in the spirit of making learning interesting, do we deal with essential topics students do not like?

There are two things we can do. The first is to **spice up dull topics** and the second is to **sell students on the benefits of the new learning**. Let's consider the first: When we cook bland meat, we add spice to give it pizzazz. If its flavor is not the best, we cover it with savory sauce. If it looks drab, we give it a colorful garnish. We can do the same with important topics that otherwise make students groan, sigh, and gaze at the clock. We do this by taking something students like, such as physical movement, and working it into a topic they don't much like, such as learning parts of speech.

Here are some of the things students like. With a little imagination, one or more can be used to add fun to almost any dull topic:

- Movement
- Novelty
- Mystery
- Adventure
- Drama
- Storytelling
- Challenge
- Role-playing or acting out
- Music and rhythm
- Field trips
- Guest speakers

Primary teachers sometimes have students clap, hop, and chant when learning number facts. They tell stories that include new reading and spelling words. Teachers of older students use challenges such as, "I bet you can't get this work done in under 10 minutes." They have students act out the functions of parts of speech, let them role-play the duties of government officials, or take field trips to local government offices where officials describe their duties.

The second way to get students to participate in dull topics is to sell students on the benefits of the new learning. Jack Collis has written a popular book on how companies ought to treat customers. It is called *When Your Customer Wins, You Can't Lose* (1998). He says people buy products for only two reasons—either to fill a need or to make themselves feel better. Perhaps you don't want to think of yourself as a salesperson trying to sell students on learning. But as Collis suggests, you can't lose in teaching if your students feel that what they get is worthwhile. Collis says the way to sell people anything is to show how they benefit from it. He says if customers could express how they'd like to be treated, they would say,

> Sell me ideas, a better self-image, freedom from fear and want, and a philosophy of life that will enable me to grow and reach my potential as a human being. Don't just sell me products or services. (1998, p. 111).

When we take that approach with students, when we explain the benefits of what we offer them, they will comply with most of our wishes. They will study even the dullest topics for a while, provided we earn their trust and use our charismatic powers of explanation and persuasion.

5. When Appropriate, Consider Using a Facilitative Style of Teaching

The majority of teachers, most of the time, use a directive style of teaching. If you have a class of highly motivated students eager to learn the material, directive teaching is the most efficient of all methods. You know what students need to learn. You organize interesting activities that enable them to learn quickly. You give direct input, provide assistance, and correct errors to help students progress. There is no better way of teaching, provided students make a sincere effort to learn. But as we have seen too well, great numbers of today's students don't make a strong effort to learn much of what we try to teach them. Teachers who believe they can simply tell students what to do and then have the students comply are lost before they begin. They do not understand they can't make students want to learn, but can only entice them with attractive possibilities. Here is how most directive teachers teach.

- Organize the learning tasks and set the standards
- Explain and demonstrate, then make assignments
- Rarely ask for student input on topics or work preferences
- Grade students' work and point out what they have done wrong.
- Use coercion attempting to force student compliance

If you use this style of teaching—and it can be very good indeed—but find that your students resist it and misbehave in doing so, consider using a facilitative approach. It often produces better results because it is attuned to students' needs and preferences. Facilitative teachers involve students closely in the instructional process and tap into their intrinsic motivation. They spend most of their time on two things: organizing interesting activities and providing assistance. They typically do the following (this is not very effective in early primary grades):

- Discuss the curriculum with the class in such a way that many topics of interest are identified.
- Encourage students to identify topics they would like to explore in depth.
- Discuss with students how they might undertake their work and suggest some possibilities.
- Identify resources that might be needed, what the students intend to accomplish, and the amount of time they will require.

AN EXAMPLE OF DIRECTIVE TEACHING   Mr. Márquez, a very well organized teacher who uses a directive style of teaching, introduces his unit on South American geography in this way:

> Class, today we are going to begin our study of the geography of South America. We are going to learn many interesting things about that fascinating part of the world. You will be expected to do the following:
>
> **1.** Learn the names of the South American countries.
> **2.** Locate those countries on a blank map.
> **3.** Describe the types of terrain typical of each country.

4. Describe the lifestyles and customs of the people of each country.
5. Name two products associated with each country.
6. Describe the population of each country in terms of ethnic origin and economic well-being.
7. Name and locate the most important rivers that drain to the north, east, and southeast.

We will learn this information from our textbooks, encyclopedias, other reference books, and selected videos. You will have two tests, one at . . .

AN EXAMPLE OF FACILITATIVE TEACHING   To see how facilitative teaching contrasts with directive teaching, note how Mr. García introduces his unit on South America geography:

Class, have any of you ever lived in South America? You did, Samuel? Which country? Perú? Fantastic! What an interesting country. I once lived in Brazil. I traveled in the Amazon and stayed with Indians for a while. They were headhunters at one time, but not now. Later I'll show you a bow and arrow I brought from that tribe. Samuel, did you ever eat monkey when you were in Perú? I think Perú and Brazil are very alike in some ways but very different in others. What was Perú like compared to here? Did you get up into the Andes? They have fabulous ruins all over Perú, I hear, and those fantastic Chariots of the Gods lines and drawings on the landscape. Do you have any photographs or slides you could bring for us to see? What a resource you can be! You can teach us a lot!

Class, Samuel lived in Perú and traveled in the Andes. If we could get him to teach us about that country, what do you think you would like to learn? (The class discusses this option and identifies topics.) We have the opportunity in our class to learn a great deal about South America, its mountains and grasslands, its dense rain forests and huge rivers, and its interesting people and strange animals. Did you know there are groups of English, Welsh, Italians, and Germans living in many parts of South America, especially in Argentina? Did you know there are still thought to be tribes of Indians in the jungles who have no contact with the outside world? Did you know that almost half of all the river water in the world is in the Amazon basin, and that in some places the Amazon River is so wide that from the middle you can't see either shore?

Speaking of the Amazon, I swam in a lake there that contained piranhas, and look, I still have my fingers and toes. Surprised about that? If you wanted to learn more about living in the Amazon jungle, what would you be interested in knowing? (Discussion ensues.)

How about people of the high Andes? Those Incas, for example, who in some mysterious way cut and placed enormous boulders into gigantic, perfectly fitting fortress walls? Samuel knows about them. The Incas were very civilized and powerful, with an empire that stretched for three thousand miles. Yet they were conquered by a few Spaniards on horseback. How in the world could that have happened? If you could learn more about those amazing people, what would you like to know? (Discussion continues in this manner. Students identify topics they would like to learn about.)

Now let me see what you think of this idea: I have written down the topics you said you were interested in, and I can help you find resources and materials. I have some of my own I can lend you, including slides, South American music, and several artifacts. I know two people who lived in Argentina and Colombia that we could invite to talk with us. We can explore what interests you. I'll help as I can and you, for your part, will agree to do the best work you are capable of. What do you think? Want to give it a try?

IN REVIEW: PUTTING IT ALL TOGETHER

Students say school is boring. They hate doing boring activities and resist through misbehavior when we try to make them. We can correct that situation by providing learning activities that are consonant with students' natures and capabilities, their needs, and their learning preferences.

We have seen that students have clearly identifiable needs which they attempt to satisfy in school. To the best of your ability, make sure their needs are met in your classes. Once again, those needs are for:

1. *Security*—to feel safe physically and psychologically.
2. *Hope*—to retain the belief that the future holds new challenges and opportunities.
3. *Dignity*—to maintain a positive, competent sense of self.
4. Acceptance—to be acknowledged, prized, and feel a member of the group.
5. *Power*—to have some control over events that affect them personally.
6. *Enjoyment*—to engage in activities that are pleasurable and rewarding.
7. *Competence*—to know and understand and be able to do things well.

Students differ in how they prefer to work at instructional tasks. To the best of your ability, make sure students are allowed to learn in ways they prefer. Steer clear of activities and procedures they dislike. Students **like** to work in the ways that involve:

- Talking with others
- Moving about
- Productive and creative work

- Use of hands
- Group work projects
- Cooperative work
- Team competition
- Efforts to surpass personal levels of achievement
- Use of computers and media equipment
- Language that has rhythm, rhyme, and metaphor
- Stories
- Role-playing, skits, and other performances
- Rhythmic activities with repetition, music, chanting, clapping, and dancing

They do **not** like:

- Sitting still for long periods
- Keeping quiet for long periods
- Working by themselves
- Memorizing facts for tests
- Lengthy writing assignments
- Repetitive busy work
- Long reading assignments
- Individual competition where the same few students always come out on top

Students find certain topics fascinating but try to avoid others. We teachers have a fairly good idea which is which, but the way to be sure is to allow students a strong say in what they want to study. The curriculum guide is a good place to start. Name topics it contains and let students give their reactions. Let them suggest a few alternative topics they might like to explore in depth. Let them decide whom they want to sit by and work with. Let them decide on time needed for completing assignments and what they will show as evidence of completion.

A directive teaching style is very effective with students who are highly motivated, but when students have little motivation a facilitative style obtains better involvement. When you allow students to participate in decisions that affect the group, they become much more willing to cooperate and conduct themselves properly. You can let them decide on some of the topics they want to learn about and how to pursue them. You can suggest possible resources and let them decide what kind of help they require. For the most part, you will be happy with the results. When you are not, discuss your concerns with the students.

Where Do We Go from Here?

We have given attention to the first five elements that contribute to class synergy. It is your responsibility to put these five elements in place. We are now ready to consider the remaining four elements.

Collaboration between you and your students is necessary for putting these four elements in place. The next element we will consider is *class agreements*. These are decisions made jointly by you and your students concerning how everyone will work and behave in the classroom.

To Think About

1. In your view, which ones of the seven student needs are easiest to meet in the classroom? Which are most difficult to meet? Why do so many teachers allow student needs to go unmet?
2. Why do you think so many of today's students say school is not worthwhile? To what extent do you think you will be able to help students enjoy school? Realistically, what success rate would you be satisfied with—70 percent of your students? 85 percent? More?
3. Directive and facilitative teaching were contrasted. Directive teaching is clear, precise, and to the point. Facilitative teaching is fuzzy in comparison—teachers do not know exactly how they will proceed, how students will react, or what the result will be. Recognizing that, do you think most teachers would want to try facilitative teaching? Why or why not?
4. Think back to your own days in school. What was the dullest topic you can remember—one that you had to make yourself suffer through? If you had to teach that topic, how do you think you could (a) make it fairly interesting for students and (b) persuade students the topic is really worth their time and effort?
5. For a grade level of your preference, see if you can outline (a) what students are like, (b) what their needs are, and (c) how they prefer working. Now outline how you would teach in a way that gives maximum attention to student nature, needs, and preferred ways of working.

6

CLASS AGREEMENTS THAT HELP EVERYONE LEARN, HAVE FUN, AND GET ALONG

Excelent thinking, Children! Unfortunately, "Eat ice cream at 9:30" and "Call for pizza at 12:00" are not exactly what we mean by class agreements.

SIXTH-GRADE TEACHER: DAVID BALLANTYNE

David Ballantyne describes how he establishes class agreements with his students:

On the first day of school, I greet my new students, introduce myself, and tell them I am pleased to see them. I say warmly (and mean it) that I am looking forward to knowing and working with them. I tell them that I am sure we will have an excellent year together and learn a great deal. I assure them I will do all I can to make the year enjoyable and that I intend to have an enjoyable time myself.

I take a few minutes to acquaint them with school rules about running in the corridors and where to cross the street. I make sure they know the locations of our playground, restrooms, cafeteria-auditorium, library, and the secretary's office and nurse's station. I then spend about an hour exploring how they would like our class to function.

My classroom has moveable tables that can be rearranged easily. I show the students how to place them in a circle so we can all see each other. We practice doing that quickly and quietly. I sit in the circle with the students. I tell them this is how we will sit for meetings to discuss class business. I tell them that when in the circle everyone has the right to speak and we will hear everyone out, in turn, without interrupting. I say this is the place where we will decide how to make our class the best it can possibly be and that we are now going to begin deciding how to do precisely that.

I ask them to tell me, without mentioning any names, some of the things they have *not* liked about school in the past year or two, things for us to avoid. Their comments usually include the following:

- People being mean to you on the playground and cafeteria (verbal abuse, teasing, taunting, put-downs)
- Too much homework
- Nothing interesting to do (no fun, talk, laughing, or neat stuff)
- Stupid assignments (boring, busy work, too much reading)
- Mean teachers (demanding, unreasonable, unfriendly, grouchy)
- Put-downs by teachers and other students in the class (sarcasm, name-calling)
- Not being listened to or allowed to discuss or express opinions

I keep a chart beside me and list their comments. I assure them I don't want any of those things they have mentioned to be present in our class. But I say we will need to work together to keep them out.

Next I ask them to tell me some of the things they *have liked* about school in the past year or two (again, no names). They mention many isolated cases of kindness and things they have enjoyed. After a time they focus in on the following:

- Being with your friends (talk, play, work together, enjoy each other's company)
- Fun activities (sports, art, performances)
- Nice teachers (friendly, helpful, understand when you make a mistake, don't make you feel bad or punish you)

I write these things on the chart and tell them that with their help I will do my best to see we have those things in our room.

I move on to say that sometimes there are things in classes that I don't like either and I hope they will help make our class good for me. Instead of listing my concerns as dissatisfactions I list them as my needs, which I write on the chart alongside what students like about school:

- Considerate behavior (I define this as everyone in the room being polite, kind, and helpful to each other.)
- Student responsibility in learning (I define this as paying attention, participating, and completing assignments.)
- High-quality work (I define this as work you'd be proud to show others.)

- Fairly low level of noise (just one of my personal needs, I explain.)

For each of my needs, I give a positive and negative example to help explain what I mean.

At this point, we take a break or go out for recess. When we come back we get in the circle and review what we have said we like, dislike, and need in school. I ask them if we can come up with some agreements about how we will all conduct ourselves in the room. The agreements should meet their needs and mine. We compare the lists and before long decide that one agreement would be to respect everyone and be kind and polite and not tease or call people names. We decide another agreement could have to do with class work. Other agreements are considered and we typically end up with around five:

1. Every person in the class—teacher and student alike—will always show consideration and respect for everyone else.
2. All class activities and assignments will be made as enjoyable as possible.
3. Every student in the class will take responsibility for doing high-quality work.
4. The teacher will always be helpful to students.
5. When we have concerns and disagreements we will work them out in a polite way, either personally or by discussing them in class meetings.

To discuss our agreements, I give example scenarios about student squabbles, disrespectful student and teacher behavior, and holding grudges. I ask the class whether in those scenarios our agreements are being followed or violated. We discuss ways of resolving the problems. I tell them that later we will learn a way to settle disagreements in a polite way (win-win conflict resolution which I teach later).

I end this session by thanking them for their excellent thinking and asking this question: "Do you ever see drivers speeding—driving well over the speed limit?" They all say they do. I then say, "The speed limits are agreements that most people consider wise and important. And yet those agreements are sometimes broken. In our class, I know you consider our agreements wise and important, yet there may be times when they are broken. For your homework tonight, I'd like you to write out four suggestions concerning what we ought to do when someone breaks one of our agreements."

The next day, students share and discuss their suggestions concerning how to deal with violations of agreements. Most of their suggestions are unrealistic or counterproductive, such as the following:

- Make them (the violators) stay in after school.
- Send them to the principal's office.
- Make them do extra work.

- Make them sit in the back of the room.
- Make them apologize.

I remind the students of our first agreement, which is to show consideration and respect for everyone. I ask what we might do, or what I might do, that would be helpful and respectful to students who break the agreements. This question really causes students to think. It is hard for them to come up with much besides the following:

- You could warn us that we are breaking a rule and need to stop.
- You could talk with students who break rules.
- Maybe we could remind each other.

I tell them that sometimes I might make a mistake without intending to. I ask them what should be done if I inadvertently violate one of the agreements by giving a boring lesson or speaking harshly to a student. They think hard about that, too. They usually say: "We could remind you and you would change it or stop." I say to them, "If I ever do that, I may catch myself and apologize. If I don't, I want you to tell me right then." I end the second day's session by thanking them for the helpful ideas they have come up with.

The next day I show students an attractive chart I have posted in the room that contains class agreements, abbreviated as follows:

Our Class Agreements

1. Courtesy and Respect at All Times
2. Enjoyable Activities and Assignments
3. High Quality Work in a Neat Classroom
4. Continual Helpfulness From the Teacher
5. Problems Solved in a Polite, Respectful Way

I point out that the chart says nothing about what will be done when anybody breaks an agreement. I tell them we will always do what agreement #5 says—work the problem out in a polite, respectful way.

At the end of the day, I give students copies of the agreement typed out in full. I ask them to sign the copy and take it home for their parents to see. I ask them to explain the agreements to their parents and ask parents to sign the copy and return it.

Thereafter, we refer to our agreements regularly. When I see violations, I whisper to the student that the class needs his or her help. If violations are repeated, I explore with the class to see if they understand why the agreements are being broken and ask if perhaps we need to change the agreement in some way. I conduct occasional practice activities in which we role-play abiding by or violating the agreements. In some of these, I have the teacher violate an agreement and ask students what they think should be done.

MAKING AND USING CLASS AGREEMENTS

Teachers have long known that when students participate in making decisions they become more likely to abide by them. Rudolf Dreikurs and Pearl Cassel (1972) were among the first to suggest teachers should allow "shared responsibility" with students. Later, Thomas Gordon (1989) pushed for participative classroom management where teachers share power and decision making with their students. William Glasser (1993) was influential in urging teachers to ask for student input that would lead to motivation and quality work. Their advice is sound, but how do we begin? You might consider Mr. Ballantyne's approach:

1. Ask students what they enjoy most about school. Usually they will mention friends, sports, art, music, and working on projects. You may get additional responses. Write what they say on a chart or the chalkboard. As a group, discuss the ideas and consolidate them. Point out that everyone doesn't have to agree—some people like one thing and others like something different. When that is done, tell them that with their help you will do your best to provide what they like best.

2. Ask students what they dislike most about school. You can expect them to name homework, boring work, busy work, working alone, being intimidated and being scolded or punished. They usually will have much to say. As they make their responses, don't be defensive or think you need to set them straight. Take note of their responses and consolidate them. Tell the students that with their help you will do the best you can to see that things they dislike do not occur in the class.

3. Ask students what they like in teachers. Or ask them what good teachers do. Usually they will mention being nice, kind, enthusiastic, funny, friendly, interesting, organized, helpful, interested in you, stick by you, talk to you, and don't make you feel bad when you make mistakes. Ask them what they don't like for teachers to do. (Scold, punish, speak sarcastically, act sour, give you bad grades). Write what they say. When that is done tell them you will always treat them with respect, keep a sense of humor, help them however you can, and try never under any circumstances to belittle them or treat them cruelly.

4. Ask students how they prefer to work in the class. Or ask what kinds of class work they enjoy most. If they have difficulty responding, ask

   - Do you prefer working alone or with friends?
   - Do you like lots of activity or do you prefer quiet work?
   - Do you like to work on projects where you develop or construct something?
   - Do you like planning and putting on special events (such as plays, science nights, writers' conferences, athletic performances, and the like)?

Tell them that with their help, you will do your best to provide interesting lessons that allow them to work in ways they prefer.

5. Ask them how they would like members of this class to behave. It may be helpful to ask questions such as:

- How do good friends treat you? Do they hurt you? Frighten you? Speak cruelly to you? Embarrass you? What do they do? (Expect the following responses: They are kind to you, support you and stick by you.)
- How do you treat your good friends? (The same as above)
- What do some students do that frightens you or makes you feel bad? (Call you names, bully you, pick on you, tease you, yell at you, and take things from you) Write what they say. Ask if they would like to make an agreement to treat others in the class well, and never badly. (They will say yes.) Tell them that you also want the class to be very much as they have suggested. Thank them sincerely for their many fine suggestions. Tell them you will write out what they have said and will have further discussion about it tomorrow. You may need to spread this out over three or four days.

Before the next day or days, consolidate what students have said about:

- School and class (how they want the class to be)
- Teachers (how they want you to behave and teach)
- Class activities (kinds of instructional activities they prefer)
- Class behavior (how students and teacher should conduct themselves)

Make a separate chart or overhead transparency for each topic. One way to do this is to list "likes" down one side, "dislikes" down the other, and leave space at the bottom where statements of agreement can be added. Here is an example for agreements about class activities:

Our Feelings about Class Activities

What We Like	What We Dislike
Interesting things to do	Boring work, it's the worst
Let us work together	Busy work for no purpose
Let us talk while working	Always working by ourselves
Make some things we can show others	Not allowed to talk or laugh
	Red marks all over our papers
Give us some quiet time too	

Our Agreement about Activities

The next day, show the chart or overhead to the students. Ask them to review it and make changes if appropriate. When that is done, ask them if they think we as a class can write some agreements about how we prefer class activities to be. Jot students' ideas on a separate chart and then put them into statements to be added beneath the heading "Our Agreements about Activities." Examples of agreements might be:

- All activities will be made as interesting as possible. Students will be the judge.
- Only work of importance will be assigned. There will be no busy work.
- Students can talk and move about except in activities designated as "quiet work"
- All activities will be purposeful—making a product or learning skills or information.

When you and the students are satisfied with the agreements, you can add them to the chart which is displayed in the classroom. The chart can be used regularly to appraise lessons. It is understood that all agreements can be modified when necessary.

Follow the same procedure to arrive at agreements concerning how students will behave and how you will teach and treat students. These agreements should be displayed in the classroom and used regularly to evaluate instruction and behavior. If you change classrooms during the day, keep the agreements on small charts or overhead transparencies (tastefully done) that you carry with your other materials.

PRIVATE COMMUNICATION

While class meetings are intended to encourage frank expression of ideas and concerns, they are not effective with all students. Some kids are too shy to speak out. Some are fearful of what classmates might say or think about them and others are burdened with matters too private or intense for open discussion. You should arrange a time for private talks where students can chat about school matters or express concerns they are reluctant to mention publicly. Occasionally students are laboring with difficult situations at home and may need a sympathetic ear. You should not ask about home matters that might be touchy—students may think you are prying and many parents take offense if asked about their private lives. Speaking with all students is easy for elementary teachers but difficult for high school teachers because of the number of students involved. There, private talks can be conducted when other students are doing seatwork, or you might make yourself available at noon or after school. Or you might encourage students to write you notes. You will find private talks and notes helpful not only for ideas you get from students but also for the role that communication plays in building trust.

Additional Examples of Class Agreements

Kindergarten

Marilyn Kimbell describes how she gets things under way with her kindergarten students who are not able to reason as older students do.

For kindergartners, the first day of school is often their first time away from mother—and the first time mother is away from her child. (Only very rarely does a father brings the child to school the first day, so here I will call the parent mother.) The first few minutes are crucial for success and may set the tone for a long time to come. A weeping mother needs a compassionate teacher as much or more than does the nervous child. To help this process, I obtain my class list before school starts and send each child a handwritten, personally addressed postcard. I select cards with pictures of animals. This breaks the ice with the child and parents and does wonders to establish initial rapport. It helps everyone feel that I care about the child and am not a total stranger.

When the children arrive on the first day, I introduce myself and assure both the child and parent that we are going to have a very nice time together. I gently encourage the mother to leave as quickly as possible, explaining that this helps the child settle down.

As I greet the children, I ask them if they can find their name tag among those I have spread out on a table. The tags have a string that students slip on over their heads with the name in front. I have two sixth-grade student assistants to help the children find their names and get them their tags on properly.

Either my assistants or I then help the child find something interesting to do. At different places in the room I have set out puzzles, dolls, blocks, Legos®, and a completely furnished playhouse large enough for the children to go inside it. Outside are swings and a large sandbox. We tell the children to play (they are supervised) until I ring the bell, then they are to come to me. I show them the bell.

When I ring the bell, I show the children how to line up at the door. This takes some teaching because most do not know how to do it.

When they are properly lined up, I ask them to come in and sit on the circle, which I have previously drawn on the carpet. I have placed tags with their names where I want them to sit. I teach them to follow around the circle, find their place, and sit down. (I assign places in the circle and seating at the tables to let each student know they have a special place that belongs only to them.) I inform them this is the way we will always come into the room. Every time we go out for recess or lunch we line up and return to the circle in this same way. I ask children what they think might happen if we all tried to crowd into the room at the same time. They understand they might hurt each other or bump into each other. I also explain that we enter this way so they can always see me and I can always see them. I smile and say it is important to me to see their smiling faces when they enter. This reassures them of their importance and helps set a pleasant tone.

When we first come to the circle, I quickly review the basic safety rules concerning pushing, hitting, jumping out of the swings, and throwing sand. I ask them what might happen if we push, hit, or throw sand. They understand the dangers and I ask, "Can we all agree never to do those things?" They answer yes. The first time we get ready to go out to the playground I ask them if they can remember our agreements about how to behave. They are usually able to repeat them. I say, "I will be keeping my eyes open to see who remembers to follow our agreements." I watch and compliment those who conduct themselves safely.

A sense of fair play is a high priority for kindergarten students so they have no trouble understanding why we raise our hands before speaking. I ask them to close their eyes and imagine what would happen if we wanted to tell about what we did yesterday and everybody tried to talk at the same time. They get the point and I say I have a suggestion—let's raise our hands before speaking in the circle. That way, only one person talks at a time and everyone gets a turn. I ask them to think of their dog, or if they don't have one to pretend they do. I say I want them to tell me the color of their dog. I ask them what they should do before speaking. I raise my hand to remind them and most raise theirs. Some blurt out anyway. I only call on those who raise their hands and thank them for remembering. It doesn't take others long to get the idea.

I mentioned the assigned seating to help students have a sense of "place" in the room. I also use seating to help them understand they "belong" to our class. When students are absent, I look at the vacant place at tables and the circle and say, "We don't have our whole group. We need Sally." This helps them see that everyone is important.

The next time we are at the circle I ask if other children sometimes do things that make them feel bad. They usually mention getting pushed, someone talking mean to them or taking what they are playing with. I ask them if we might be able to agree never to push, talk mean to someone else, or take something away from another. We discuss better ways of treating each other. I make the examples concrete: "Jason, suppose that Anthony is ahead of you in line and you feel like pushing him and getting in front. But we have agreed not to push. What would be a better thing for you to do?" or "Heather, suppose María is playing with the Raggedy Ann doll and you want it. But we have agreed not to take things away from others. What could you do that would be better?" We discuss such options as waiting for our turn, locking our lips when we feel like saying something mean, or asking others if we can play with them. We review these agreements regularly. Students quickly begin calling attention to class members who break the agreements.

We also talk from time to time about materials and activities the children like best, such as playing with the toys, coloring, listening to stories, watching videos, singing, and listening to children's music. I keep careful tabs on what they say so I can make sure to include their preferences regularly. When I see certain things children do not enjoy, I delete them from my program. From time to time I introduce a new activity to add variety and broaden children's interests.

I do not ask my students how they would like teachers to treat them. They don't yet have sufficient experience. I simply make a point of treating them well. I believe by modeling gentle, polite behavior, I help them behave that way as well. I know at home many are regularly punished, yelled at, belittled, and allowed to run about wildly and bully others. I can't change the world but I feel I can make a difference for my students at school. I always treat them kindly and respectfully. I remind them of our agreements when I see them behaving rudely. We spend time reflecting on how we like to be treated and why it is best to treat others the same way. When students' minds wander, I gently remind them of the "jobs" all of us must do if we are to learn and enjoy ourselves. I do not use punitive measures. They are not necessary. Reminders suffice and the need for them diminishes as the school year progresses. Whispering a reminder just to the child who needs it helps preserve the child's self-image. Trust grows as I show I will never embarrass them in front of others or frighten them but will instead be kind and helpful. I have found that when students like and trust me, I only need to ask for their help. They give it gladly.

Third Grade
Teacher Talli Sunday brings students into the planning process in the following manner:

After six years of teaching third grade I have a pretty good idea of what my students need educationally, what kinds of activities they enjoy most, and how they like teachers to treat them. I involve students in planning most of what we do in the class, not because I think they will reveal anything new to me (though occasionally they do) but for two other reasons. First, I want them to feel more involved in their educational process and I want to help them understand the process better, especially why certain topics and activities are used and why certain kinds of behavior improve learning. Second, I want them to see that good education is something teachers and students do together, not just something teachers do to students.

My Students' Needs   When I begin the year I have in mind a list of what I feel my students need educationally. I don't mention the list to the students. I use it to guide the discussion we have right after I have oriented them to the school and classroom and helped them get comfortable. My list of educational needs for students is as follows:

1. To learn interesting and useful information, especially that which promotes skills in reading, math, and language.
2. A learning environment that is attractive, stimulating, free from threat, and conducive to productive work.

3. A teacher who is attentive, helpful, and kind.
4. The opportunity to work and interact cooperatively with other students.
5. To be accepted and feel part of the group.
6. To learn how to relate to others humanely and helpfully.

I begin the discussion by telling them third grade is an important and wonderful year in their lives. They will learn some new things that will make them feel proud, such as cursive handwriting like high school students use and how to do multiplication in math and how to read new and interesting books. I then draw their attention to the classroom. I ask if they have ever seen a classroom when it is vacant in the summer, with nothing inside it, no tables, chairs, books, pictures, or materials of any kind. (A few say they have. I ask others to imagine it.) I ask what they see in this room that is different from a bare room. (I have the room neatly arranged with an attractive bulletin board, books, toys and puzzles, maps, globe, growing plants, aquarium, a carpeted reading corner, a science learning center, and a display of art work done by previous students.) They spend some time noticing these things. After a bit I ask, "Why do you suppose all these things are in the room? What is their purpose? Why don't we just have a bare room, like this room is in summer?"

This gets across the idea that the materials are there for a specific purpose, not just something that comes with all classrooms. I tell them I need their help in one matter: I am not sure which of the things we have noticed in the room they will like best. I need to find that out from them personally. I say they won't really know, themselves, until they've worked with the materials, but for now what do they think? Someone always says they like the aquarium and I ask, "What do you think we might learn from the aquarium?" I use further leading questions to open up possibilities that do not occur to them.

My Needs   I have needs concerning the classroom, student attitude, and student behavior. I am open about my needs and discuss them with the students. I tell them I will do everything I can to make school enjoyable for them and hope they will do the same for me. I tell them these are the things I need to make school good for me:

1. An attractive but orderly classroom. I like to have beautiful and useful things in the room but need them to be neat. I can't stand working in a mess of strewn papers, tumbled books, and upended chairs. I need the materials to be neatly stored, I like the displays to be in good order, and I need clutter kept off the floor. I ask students if they feel they can help me with that. They invariably say they can.
2. Student cooperation. I need my students to work with me. I need them to pay attention, listen to other speakers, and follow directions. I don't want them to squabble or be disagreeable. I

tell them I will always treat them with kindness and respect and ask if they feel they can give that to other students and me in return. They naturally say they can.

3. Enthusiasm from everyone. I assure them I will provide interesting activities and I'd like for them to show enthusiasm. I explain what enthusiasm means.

4. A warm pleasant classroom atmosphere, where everyone is polite and helpful. I tell them I know they may not always feel kind and polite, but part of becoming educated is learning how to control our feelings so we don't treat others badly when we feel bad.

In a discussion usually on the second day of class, I ask students how they would like their fellow students to behave and especially how they would like to be treated by others. I say, "To begin with, what *don't* you like for them to do?" Their responses are fairly standard: nobody push or try to fight me, nobody call me names, nobody tease me, nobody take things that belong to me. I list these things on the board and ask, "Well, if you don't like these, how *do* you want others to treat you?" Again their predictable responses are: be nice, don't call names, don't push, don't fight, don't take my things. I tell them I don't like those things either, so I wonder if we can all agree that we won't do any of them—no pushing, no fighting, no name calling, no taking other people's things. They nod and say yes. I tell them it makes me very happy to know they like a kind classroom just as I do.

Then I tell them there are two things we haven't discussed that I dislike very much and wonder if they can help me with them. The things I mention are:

- Too much noise from loud voices, loud laughing, and scraping of chairs and tables.
- Defacing or destroying property, such as books and instructional materials.

Class Understandings   On the following day, I tell students I believe we have come to an understanding about how we want the class to be and how we want to behave. I remind them that some of the ideas are theirs and some are mine. I have written the following on a chart. We go over the items and for each we discuss what we believe it means.

1. Be polite and considerate of others at all times. (Speak kindly. Be helpful. Don't be rude to others or bother them.)

2. Do our best work. (Get as much done as we can. Do our work neatly so we can be proud of it. Don't waste time.)

3. Use quiet voices in the classroom. (Use regular speaking voices during class discussions. Speak quietly during cooperative work groups. Whisper at other times if you need help.)

4. Take care of the room and contents. (Keep it clean and tidy. Don't ruin materials.)

I end by assuring them that I will do my best to be polite, enthusiastic, and helpful, and that I will always listen to their concerns. I ask them to help me in return by being cooperative and doing work they feel proud of.

Ongoing   As time passes I try to make every student feel secure and wanted. I try to keep thing lively. I give students lots of smiles, winks, nods, and pats. Sometimes I tell them how pleased I am with the way they are working or behaving toward each other. I thank them for helping make the class enjoyable for me. Once in a while, when the whole class has behaved especially well, I give them a special reward such as going early to recess, doing one of their favorite activities such as art, or watching a special video. From time to time I send complimentary notes to their parents or call the students on the phone to comment on how well they are doing. I like to talk with them in ways that imply their competence, such as, "Okay, you know what to do next." I end each day on a positive note, with a fond good-bye and hopes for a happy and productive tomorrow.

Grade 10 English
Teacher Gail Jones describes a change in teaching she felt she had to make in order to preserve her professional integrity.

I have been teaching for 23 years in the same school. I enjoyed it in the beginning; my students were considerate and motivated. For the most part they did what I asked and they learned well. If they misbehaved I controlled them with facial expressions and reminders. As the years passed, society changed and so did the students in my school. They no longer seemed much interested in what I tried to teach them. I pushed hard but with little result. I began to lecture students about courtesy and responsibility and the need to make something of themselves. I used threat and detention to get them to do what they were supposed to. That brought grudging compliance but never any excitement. I knew students no longer liked my classes. I didn't enjoy them either, nor the students. Every day left me exhausted. I longed for weekends and dreaded Monday mornings.

Three years ago I realized I could no longer fight this losing battle and would have to find a way out of it or do something else for a living. I had been a demanding teacher with high standards. That was fine at first, but now students wouldn't respond to the demands. For my sake more than theirs, I decided I'd have to find a more peaceful way of teaching. I hated to give up the challenging curriculum I was proud of but knew it wouldn't fly unless I could make it very attractive to students. I had learned the hard way I couldn't force them through the paces any more.

A New Approach   I spent the summer thinking about how I might make a new attempt at teaching. I realized that the closeness I once experienced with students was no longer present. I decided to try to recapture that, at least. If I could, I figured I'd be able to teach my course. If I couldn't, I'd better call it quits. I still believed high school students wanted to be on good terms with their teachers even when they didn't act like it. I knew they wanted someone to trust, to model themselves after, and to feel safe with. I decided to try being such a person.

I had always greeted new students at the beginning of the year with two things—an overview of the class (the demands of which dismayed them, I realized) and printed rules of class behavior and consequences for breaking the rules. In early years, students accepted both. Now they considered them impositions. That was the first thing I changed. When I meet them now I introduce myself and tell some things about my life, interests, and family. I reveal myself as a human rather than taskmistress. I don't say much about the class at first. I tell them I have been worried that school doesn't help students as it ought to and I'd like to see that change. I admit that English is a class that students usually don't enjoy very much. I tell them I want to change that and perhaps can do so if they help. I suggest we talk about how we might accomplish it. I place a chart on an easel beside me. It contains the following questions:

1. When have you felt most successful in school?
2. What did the teacher do to help you feel successful?
3. What kinds of class activities have you found most helpful and enjoyable?
4. What suggestions do you have for creating a classroom in which all can work, learn, and do their best?

I ask them to think about the first question for a moment and jot down notes if they wish. I then allow them to share their answers. I encourage everyone to speak. On my clipboard I jot down what they say. At times I read it back and ask if I have it right. By the end of the period we have usually discussed the first three questions. I tell them that I will think deeply about what they have said and give them feedback the next day. I ask them, for their homework, to copy question #4 and do some serious thinking about it. I want to hear their ideas the next day and use them to make decisions about the class.

The next day, I organize students into small groups to share and discuss their conclusions. Volunteers present each group's responses. I list them on the overhead. Occasionally I add a suggestion of my own. We streamline, combine, reword, and sometimes negotiate until the statements satisfy everyone. Before the next class, I type up the statements for review and give everyone a copy. I do this for each of my five classes. The agreements turn out to be quite similar from class to class. I follow up on them and make sure students see their suggestions incorporated into the class.

Giving Students a Voice in Decisions   In the days that follow I continue to give students a voice in classroom matters and listen to them. I conduct class meetings to allow students to discuss what they like least and most about the class. That puts a heck of a strain on my ego, but by being open to what they say I get better cooperation. I know they like to work with each other so I let them decide where they want to sit and with whom they want to work. They know by now I will treat them kindly and will respectfully do what I can to help them succeed.

Meeting My Needs   In an early session where I ask students to say what they like and dislike about school, I tell them some things I also like, dislike, and need. I explain my feelings are similar to theirs, that I want the class to be enjoyable and worthwhile. I tell them frankly that I need the tone in the room to be positive, with patience, tolerance, good manners, and mutual respect.

Living with the Agreements   I teach five classes of English with an average enrollment of 35. My students are easily distracted. I accept it is up to me to keep the students engaged. I find they respond best when I help them choose interesting books to read and allow them to give their reactions to the books in writing. They read what they have written and discuss their efforts in small groups. I present mini-lessons that address common writing needs evident in the class, such as constructing strong sentences and sequencing them for power and persuasion. Students are motivated to do excellent work because it will be included in "showcase portfolios" each student produces. The portfolios are put on display for parents, teachers, administrators, and visitors at a Writers' Tea that my classes organize at the end of each semester. This display has the advantage of motivating students to use correct grammar and spelling. Students use word processors in the computer lab or at home to give their work a professional appearance. I encourage them to illustrate their work and decorate their portfolios.

I make a point of interacting personally with every student. It is difficult to spend much time with each of more than 160 students, but I make sure to speak to or smile at each of them every day.

This year I decided to introduce myself to new students by means of a letter on the first day of class. It is a form letter personalized with their name. I tell about my family, hobbies, travels, interests, and so on. I ask students to write me a letter in return telling the same, to help me know them better. I keep a birthday calendar to remember their birthdays. I make a point of commenting on new hairstyles, new outfits, or how fine teeth look as they get straightened. I chaperone field trips and dances, supervise the computer writing lab after school, and make myself available for conversation with students before and after school. I find these little things mean a lot.

As I make these efforts to know and work with students, they give back respect and enthusiasm in greater degree than I had hoped. I can now guide, encourage, and support their efforts, rather than push, demand, and coerce. The power struggles have ended. Students are cooperative, happier, and more successful. The changes have definitely made me a more satisfied and more effective teacher.

Probably the most important things I have learned are: I get respect from students by first showing them respect. I get good work from them by working along with them—I want them to become good writers so I do the same assignments they do. I want them to show good manners, humor, and kindness, so I always display those qualities the best I can. I admit it when I make a mistake, and students forgive me because they know I am trying to help. Through this process I have learned the value of letting students make decisions about how they want to work and behave as a class. I give them power and respect their decisions. In turn they help me.

WHERE DO WE GO FROM HERE?

Having noted the kinds of class agreements that lead to productive relationships and attitudes, we now move ahead to the next element of synergy, a process called "coopetition." We will explore the value of coopetition, see why it is preferable in many ways to either cooperation or competition, and learn how it is implemented in the classroom.

TO THINK ABOUT

1. Teachers usually fear if they allow students to make decisions about work and behavior, standards will deteriorate. Do you think this is likely, and if so, to what extent? What might keep standards of work and conduct high when students have such power?
2. The examples in this chapter from teachers at different levels make it seem that the synergetic approach works for most all students and classes. Is this realistic? What exceptions do you see?
3. The examples all make it seem that teachers invariably get back from students what they give—that is, they get respect when they give it, good manners when they display them, and self-control when they show continual poise. Is this just a pipe dream or does it really happen? If it does happen, would it not be in varying degree? What degree would you consider acceptable? If students do not respond respectfully to teachers who show them respect, what should the teacher do? Can they not simply demand it as the authority figure in the room?

COOPETITION: COMBINING THE BEST OF COOPERATION AND COMPETITION

We have agreed on our group goal, Mrs. Córdoba, which is to thoroughly outdo ourselves.

COOPETITION: A COINED WORD

Here I find it necessary to coin a term. Or rather to use a term already coined but with a new meaning. The term has an odd sound to it. I prefer standard terms, usually plentiful within the richness of the English language. However, I couldn't find one for what we get when we combine the best of cooperation with the best of competition. The term I finally decided to use is Coopetition.[1] It is pronounced co-opetition and means **cooperating to compete.**

There has been considerable discussion in education about learning through cooperation versus through competition and some argument about which produces better results. Each has its strengths and weaknesses. Entering the twenty-first century, cooperation is the favorite of most educators. Compared to competition it produces somewhat higher achievement overall, though not necessarily for the best students. Most students enjoy it, and so when cooperating have better attitudes

---

[1] I have seen the term *coopetition* credited to Ray Noorda, founder of Novell. He used it to refer to competing companies' cooperating for mutual benefit, a meaning somewhat different from that used in this book.

toward school and cause less trouble. It seems to assist productive thinking and definitely allows better interaction among class members. Moreover, it provides a degree of motivation in that most students like to work together. But at the same time cooperation puts limits on some of the things we try to achieve in education, as we shall presently see.

Competition also has its strengths and weaknesses. In the Western World, competition is credited for producing dazzling technological advances. The early bird gets the worm. Whoever is there first gets the most. You get the best from humans, some say, when you release their energies, and the surest way to release their energy is to allow them to compete. We try to outscore the other guy, make more money, win more prizes, and climb to the top of the ladder. Being first or having the most or simply winning is the highest prize awarded in the West. In times past, great achievers worked more or less on their own without a great deal of close collaboration, as was the case with Leonardo da Vinci, Galileo Galilei, Nicolaus Copernicus, Francis Bacon, J. S. Bach, W. A. Mozart, Jeanne d'Arc, Vincent Van Gogh, Thomas Edison, the Wright Brothers, Henry Ford, Alexander Graham Bell, John Steinbeck, and so on. These people were competitive and astonishingly productive. Most writers, composers, and artists still work essentially by themselves. But how often do we see people of their creative genius? Once in a hundred thousand? What about the rest of us? Does individual competition drive our motors too?

You have to wonder. Most of us never achieve a great deal through competition. Many of us suffer because of it. At times it brings out the worst in us. As for inventions and scientific breakthroughs, they are not often credited to individuals anymore. They are made by research groups within industries and universities that stress group effort. We have think tanks where brilliant minds interact. We have seminars, work teams, and team sports. Nowadays, teamwork is the name of the game. Read the recruiting advertisements by business firms. Notice how often you see the word "team"—winning team, exciting team, teamwork, and team player. Companies look for people who can cooperate *and* be productive in large-scale enterprises.

Production from cooperation, achievement through cooperation, excellence through cooperation—this is what we strive for in synergetic teaching and discipline. In the following pages you will see why neither cooperation nor competition, by itself, adequately serves the ends of education, while a combination of the two does. In teaching, we don't reserve our energies for the single creative genius we might encounter among a lifetime of students. Our concern blankets all—the bright, the average, and the slow. Everybody is entitled to the best education we can give them. For an occasional student, the best might entail a heavy amount of competition. For an occasional student, it might involve a preponderance of cooperation. But for most of us, a combination of the two serves best.

In this chapter we will see what coopetition entails, how it is applied, and why it so often produces synergy. From fourth grade up through graduate school, coopetition is one of the best tools we have for energizing classes and helping students be productive. Unfortunately, it does not work well with primary grade students, for reasons that will be explained later.

WHAT IS GOOD AND BAD ABOUT COOPERATION

The value of cooperation in all aspects of education cannot be denied. It brings teachers and students a plethora of benefits, including:

- Enjoyment
- Quantity and divergence of ideas
- Distribution of the work load
- Better quality work product
- Learning to work together—meaning listening to others' ideas, expressing oneself persuasively, compromising, striving for solutions palatable to all
- Synergy (this is the best benefit of all)

The problem is that these benefits don't occur automatically. Sometimes cooperation produces the opposite. You can, when trying to cooperate, have a disagreeable time. You can find you do the work of two or three people, or the work of none. You may find that the product you end up with isn't much good at all. You may find that members of the group don't work well together—they don't listen, they shout, they withdraw, compromise is the last thing on their mind, and they say too bad if something doesn't please you. At times, attempting to cooperate becomes a wet blanket that smothers any hope of synergy.

I recently served on a jury deciding whether damages should be awarded to a man who claimed to have suffered irreparable neck injury and sexual impotency when his car was struck from behind on a winding road. His attorney strongly hinted that the physical suffering and mental anguish could only be recompensed by an astonishingly large sum of money. Unfortunately for the guy, a private investigator had caught him on tape in a variety of compromising activities that required, to say the least, a fit neck. We of the jury had to decide his fate. Jury deliberation is supposed to be a cooperative event in which evidence is weighed carefully. Everyone is to express their views and listen carefully to others. We had on our jury a man who made his points by shouting. He drowned out anyone whose opinion differed from his. He called their opinions stupid and their thinking haywire. He was for finding against the construction company. He was adamant the accident wouldn't have happened if road signs had been placed farther back. Myself, I thought the plaintiff was trying to seize on an easy way to make a million bucks. We finally awarded minor damages. As for the process—how we performed on that jury shows that throwing a group of people together does not ensure cooperation.

Years ago a school district I worked for wanted to consider individualizing instruction and asked me and a few strong-willed teachers to develop a workable plan. We launched into it with high expectations but before long we were in such a jumble we hardly knew which end was up. Every one of us had a different idea about what it meant to individualize instruction and how the everyday harassed teacher could manage it. I had in mind what I thought was a good plan but my colleagues shot it full of holes. After a while I didn't think much of it either, but we had a devil of a time coming up with anything better. We didn't want to admit defeat, so decided after a time to focus just on the mathematics program and see what we could do there. We managed to put a plan together, but to tell the truth it looked like the old definition of a camel—a horse designed by committee. That opinion was shared by most of the other teachers we showed it to. It was such a hodge-podge nobody could take it seriously. We had begun our work thinking six heads would be better than one but ended up well reminded that too many cooks can spoil the broth.

What Is Good and Bad about Competition

Just as cooperation has its good and bad points, so does competition. People claim that technological advances of recent decades have occurred mainly because of competition. You hear competition referred to as the engine that drives the world. People say the airplane wasn't invented by a committee (well, perhaps a committee of two), but by individuals who were trying their best to be the first to fly. People point out that the electric light wasn't invented by a cooperative group, but by a single man driven to excel, relying as he put it on one drop of inspiration and 99 drops of perspiration. Certainly there is no denying that competition has its good points, such as:

- High motivation
- Self-reliance
- Independent thought
- Assumption of responsibility
- High efficiency
- Possibility of synergy

But competition has its dark side, too, which gives us pause. It can be extremely motivating, but only for those who believe they have a chance to win. It is demoralizing for those who don't. It leads to self-reliance for those who experience occasional success, but self-reliance fades away for those who never succeed. The same goes for independent planning and assumption of responsibility. When things don't go well, competition can backfire. It puts us out all alone in the spotlight's glare, with no group to hide in. If we don't win or succeed, we can't keep it a secret. Everybody sees our shortcomings. We don't like that so we sometimes try to protect ourselves by cheating, lying, making excuses, or blaming others for our failure. There is no higher-octane fuel for synergy than competition, but it works only when hope is strong. If you know you don't have a chance of winning, competition has little allure.

COOPETITION: SEEKING THE BEST OF BOTH

In the classroom we strive for synergy, that generous goose that lays so many golden eggs. Synergy can be produced through both cooperation and competition, but each can also subvert it. In teaching, we do best when we provide most of our students with a combination of the two approaches. That brings us back to the concept of **coopetition,** cooperating in order to compete. Let's explore how that is done.

We noted that *cooperation,* at its best, gives students enjoyment, quantity and divergence of ideas, distribution of the workload, potential for a better quality product, better ability to work together, and above all synergy. On the downside cooperation can result in dissatisfaction, uneven work burden, and general boredom.

Competition at its best can bring students higher motivation, self-reliance, independent thought, assumption of responsibility, increased efficiency, and synergy. Those are qualities we hope always to preserve. The downside of competition is that it demoralizes people who feel they've no chance of winning, causes loss of self-direction and responsibility for those who never experience success, and causes us to lie and cheat to escape the sense of failure.

In *coopetition* we attempt to blend the best qualities of cooperation and competition, while eliminating their worst qualities. How we do this is shown in Figure 7.1. Coopetition is a way of working in the classroom (and elsewhere) using a combination of the best aspects of cooperation and competition. It involves competition by groups, not individuals. It can be used in a variety of instructional activities and students almost always find it motivating and enjoyable. It allows

---

1st, Merge the **upside of cooperation** with the **upside of competition.**

Enjoyment	Motivation
Quantity and divergence of ideas	Reliance on self
Distribution of the workload	Independent thinking
Better quality work product	Assumption of responsibility
Learning to work together	Increased efficiency
Synergy	Synergy

2nd, Remove the **downside of cooperation** and the **downside of competition.**

Dissatisfaction with the process	Dissatisfaction with the process
Uneven work burden	Demoralization
Lack of personal responsibility	Inclination to lie and cheat

3rd, Obtain resultant **Coopetition,** which provides for most students:

High motivation and enjoyment
Quanity and divergence of ideas
Responsibility for self within group goals
Efficient work production
Better overall quality
Strong likelihood of synergy

Figure 7.1   How cooperation and competition are blended into *coopetition.*

social exchange, leads to high achievement, gives every member important responsibility, and allows all members of the winning group to experience the heady sensation of success.

Every member of the group, regardless of competence, feels exhilarated when the group wins. They feel it fully as much as do winners of individual competition. The worst player on a team feels just as excited as the best player when the team wins and just as disappointed when it loses. If anything, teams enjoy victory more than individuals do—that comes I suppose from the camaraderie and whooping it up. A team win releases a real burst of energy.

WHEN COOPETITION IS NOT APPROPRIATE

Some instructional activities do not call for excellence or high achievement. First grade students touch and stroke a rabbit for the sole purpose of experiencing how it looks, feels, and acts. This is called an "experiential activity," and while activities of this sort are important in education, they do not call for high achievement or quality work. Certain other activities call on students to use cooperative skills but without primary emphasis on high achievement. Suppose a civics class wishes to explore firsthand some of the workings of city government and services. A cooperative group approach is used. Cooperative learning groups usually work in one of the following ways: (1) Peer instruction, where one student teaches others by tutoring or providing specific help, (2) Practice groups, where students review, drill, and check each other, (3) Investigative groups, where students work in teams to carry out investigations, or (4) Production groups, where students work in teams to produce tangible products such as models, murals, and class magazines. In our civics class example, the students work as investigative groups. One group agrees to explore the duties of mayor, council persons, and city manager. Another group agrees to explore the departments of parks and recreation, another the police force, another the fire department and city ambulance service, and so on. In consultation with the teacher, each group decides what it will try to accomplish and how it will share with the class what it learns.

The groups visit appropriate offices and in some cases invite city representatives to the class. Everyone pitches in and does their share. The primary purpose of the activity is to learn about the city, but another important objective is for students to learn to work together, share the load, and assume responsibility. Individual or group competition does not apply. It is irrelevant. The activity itself provides sufficient motivation for students to see it through and they have an enjoyable time.

As with cooperation, there are times when competitive activities are sufficient in themselves. The best of these activities involves students competing against their own past performance. They strive to increase the number of words they can spell correctly. They try to increase the number of math problems they can do in a given amount of time. Or they try to do a set number of problems in progressively shorter amounts of time. They work at improving writing skills over time and keep samples they can use to judge improvement. In physical education they try to run a given distance in less time. In auto mechanics they try to do a front disc brake replacement perfectly in less time than before. They keep records and are highly motivated to improve. These activities are for individuals only. There is no group collaboration.

There are times, too, when the best students from classes or schools meet in competition. They have spelling championships, science fairs, and contests in cooking and auto restoration. Individual competition of this type does not bring the downside effects of competition listed previously because these individuals already know they are high achievers. They have a history of excellence and are eager to test themselves against others. They are disappointed when they lose, but previous successes cushion their disappointment and help maintain their eagerness to compete.

WHEN COOPETITION IS ESPECIALLY USEFUL

From fourth grade up, coopetition provides higher levels of motivation and desire to collaborate than any other instructional approach. Its competitive side motivates all members of the group. Its cooperative side provides social engagement and the give-and-take that students enjoy. The outcomes produced through coopetition are high in quality, higher than most students can reach on their own. All students rightfully take ownership of the result.

Because continually losing is demoralizing, it is important for slower students to win competitions as frequently as faster students. This is made possible in coopetition. All members of a winning team share the sense of victory. Members of losing teams may feel disappointed, but that does not make them stop trying. They get their share of winning, too. Group competition is not nearly so likely as individual competition to cause an individual to feel like a loser.

Not all instructional activities lend themselves to coopetition. But most do. The following illustrates some of the possibilities:

Coopetition in Relation to Preset Standards

Suppose your physical education program makes use of an obstacle course in a park adjacent to the school. For the past several years you have kept records of how students have performed on the course. From those records you have established norms for male and female performers in two categories—novice and experienced. Perhaps the average ninth-grade girl new to the activity—the novice category—completes the course in 12 minutes. Ninth-grade girls who have been practicing on the course for four weeks—experienced category—complete it in an average time of 8 minutes. These are standards against which all girls in the program can compete individually. Their enthusiasm rises if you organize them into teams to see if their average times meet or surpass the standard.

You can use a similar approach in many areas of the curriculum, including topics that don't usually enthrall students, such as memorizing theorems and correct spelling. Standards of performance can be established. The standards can be organized into levels, from easier to more difficult. Students can work to meet standards and move up through levels as they improve. This can be done individually but is more effective when done in groups. It is in the group's self-interest to cooperate and help all members do their best. Performance gains can be charted to show improvement. Every person's performance should count in the group's total score. That makes everyone's contribution essential and permits all to share the sense of progress.

Coopetition Involving Groups within the Class

In the previous activity, groups competed not against each other but against preset standards. More highly motivating yet are activities in which class groups compete against each other. Group competition can be used in most areas of the curriculum. Groups should be comprised of five or six students each, the optimal size according to research in cooperative learning (Slavin, 1991). Groups should be equalized in terms of ability. Teachers can select students for the groups or assign them randomly. This gives four to six fairly equal groups for competition. Group membership should be changed from time to time.

Groups that win should do so because they work harder than the others do, not because they are more capable to begin with. If groups turn out to be noticeably different in capability, consider changing group composition as a means of equalizing them. You can level the playing field by using a system of handicapping. Just as golfers and bowlers have handicaps to permit equal competition, so can class groups. Handicapping needn't be elaborate. When a group wins a competition such as identifying the continents and oceans on a world map, they are given a minus handicap for the next competition. If performance is total score for the group, the winners might have two points deducted from their score for the next competition. If the competition is in terms of time, they might be allowed a half-minute less in the next competition. This is just like handicapping in horse racing, where the better horses have to carry more weight than the others. The point is to find a way to give every group an equal opportunity to win.

Coopetition Involving Other Classes

Students love competition against other classes or schools. Such competitions are exceptionally motivating, as evident in interscholastic sports competitions where the entire school becomes involved in the excitement. On a smaller scale, Spanish teachers Mr. Adams and Mr. Zeta agree to a competition between their classes to see which can outdo the other in vocabulary, verb conjugation, and written translation. They involve all members of the class. They allow a week for students to practice together in small groups. Motivation is high. More able students work hard to help the less able. On the appointed day, all enter into the competition as total classes, not individuals. Overall scores are obtained for each class. Everyone has contributed and shares equally in the victory or loss.

Coopetition To Exceed Expectations

As a part of their curriculum, certain classes put on regular public performances. The school band, drama classes, art classes, and, of course, athletic teams display their accomplishments as part of their normal work. Except for the athletic teams, they compete against an imaginary standard that is not even clear in their own minds—they try their best to exceed expectations they, and others, have of themselves. Many classes put on presentations of one kind or another, for back-to-school nights, assemblies, or special events such as holiday concerts and dramatic productions. Talli Sunday's third-grade classes have earned a reputation for their readers' theater performances, where students act out and read the lines of well-known stories as well as skits they compose. Other classes attend their performances in the auditorium and their evening performances draw numbers of parents and relatives. Gail Jones's Writers' Teas are a highlight of each quarter. The class invites students, parents, and relatives to the auditorium to hear students tell about their writing and read excerpts from their stories and poems. Ms. Jones notifies local media. Feature stories appear in the newspaper and occasionally on television. Marilyn Kimbell's kindergarten Thanksgiving feasts are the hit of the autumn season. Her students, their parents, and Marilyn's aide make Pilgrim and Indian costumes and hats. The kids wear the costumes and sing Thanksgiving songs for those in attendance. The parents cooperate by preparing dishes for the dinner. A number of people are invited to attend and participate in the feast and festivities. Carol Holloway's spring science fairs are popular at her school. She has students work in small groups to investigate selected topics. They prepare exhibits that describe and illustrate their work and findings. They publicize the event and extend open invitations to anyone who wishes to attend. The school auditorium is crowded with proud parents and others who examine the exhibits and talk with the student investigators.

Group activities of this sort make the best use of coopetition. Students are motivated. They work together. They carefully plan what they are to do. They accept duties and help each other. There is virtually no misbehavior. They seldom compete for prizes, but their desire to do well is strong. Throughout the process, excitement remains high and students have an enjoyable time. They take pride in what they accomplish. These activities give them an opportunity to put themselves to the test, to see what they can accomplish.

WHY COOPETITION DOESN'T WORK WELL IN THE PRIMARY GRADES

Coopetition isn't effective in the primary grades because children younger than age eight or nine do not really understand the processes of competition and cooperation. Even when you carefully explain the processes to them, they cannot act on what you say.

This begins to change at the second-grade level and by third grade many students understand the concepts and enjoy the processes. But kindergartners and first-graders are very "me" centered. If you have them work in groups you can expect the students with the most ability to take over and do the work for the whole group. It is usually the girls who do this and instead of showing the others what is needed, they do it for them. These students understand what it means to win, but they don't attach much importance to it. For example, if you have first-grade groups compete to make the best mural, they will usually color, cut, and paste as fast as they can with little regard for appearance. They may realize later that their mural is messy or not pretty, but in all likelihood they will be satisfied with it.

WHERE DO WE GO FROM HERE?

We have now given attention to seven of the nine elements that promote synergy. Activities you arrange that simultaneously allow students to cooperate *and* compete pay handsome dividends. Students find the tasks motivating. They cooperate and help each other do outstanding work. They enjoy the process and don't misbehave. You will enjoy it too.

In the next chapter we move to the eighth element of synergy, human relations. There we will examine how teachers can help students behave more politely, considerately, and humanely. We will see how to help them avoid conflict and build themselves personally through the process of accepting and respecting others.

TO THINK ABOUT

1. Coopetition has been depicted as one of the very best strategies for releasing synergy in your classroom. Do you agree? You may or may not like its competitive aspect. Can you think of other strategies that can release a similar amount of positive energy in students?

2. Select a subject and grade level you are particularly interested in. Suppose you wanted to use coopetition where your class worked to meet or surpass established standards. What subject or topic would you begin with? How would you go about

establishing the standards, organizing groups, and keeping track of group performance?

3. Suppose you want to try competition among the groups you have formed. How can you equalize them in terms of ability? Would you consider a handicap system to give all groups an equal chance to win? If so, how would you implement it? How would you explain the handicapping to students so they would understand its fairness?

4. Have you experienced group competition where all the members of your group or team worked hard to outdo another group or school? How did those experiences compare to your usual school activities in terms of excitement, cooperation with teammates, and motivation to excel?

8

HUMAN RELATIONS SKILLS: WHAT ALL OF US NEED BUT FEW EVER LEARN

No, Christine, in this particular case, 'human relations' has nothing to do with the birds and the bees.

Not long ago I went into a bank I patronized occasionally with the intention of closing my account. The account was small and I seldom used it. The bank had even changed names, so I felt even less affiliation for it than when I had first opened the account. I went inside. The tellers were occupied, so I noted a lady whose sign said she was in charge of accounts. She was busy with a client. I stood waiting, whereupon a gentleman got up from behind a desk in the far corner and came across to me. He asked if he could help me. I replied that I had come to see about closing my account. He smiled and said, "I don't know you personally, but I want to thank you for having let us be of service. I'll be glad to help you myself."

Just then the accounts lady became free. The man said, "Barbara is the expert on this. Please sit here and she will take care of you." He added as he left, "Thank you again for using our bank."

I sat down and said to Barbara, "You know, I came in today to close my account. It is so small it doesn't mean much to your bank. But that gentleman treated me so courteously, I'm having second thoughts. I think maybe I'll leave the account in place and begin using it more frequently. Who is the man, by the way?"

Barbara smiled. "That is Mr. Sowetto. He's vice president of the bank."

THIS ONE WAS NO MR. SOWETTO,

Several months ago I succumbed once again to an irrepressible urge to buy a new computer, a malady that strikes me every couple of years. When I begin to feel the urge I expect common sense to prevail, but unfortunately it never does.

I had just begun looking around and didn't know exactly what it was I so desperately needed. I thought it might be good to talk to someone in the business, so I went into a shop I had seen a number of times, thinking it would be good to speak with an expert who could make suggestions relevant to my needs. The proprietor was seated at a bench behind the counter, working at a machine with its cover off. He glanced up and nodded. He looked pleasant enough. I told him I was just beginning to think about getting myself a new computer but didn't know exactly what the latest stuff was and needed to talk with someone such as himself. He asked me when I planned to buy. I said I didn't know—in two or three months I guessed. He replied, "You're just looking around, then." I said I guessed I was, more or less.

He turned back to his work and said coldly, "Go look in the big computer outlets. They will show you everything there is and try their best to sell it to you. Once you make up your mind what you want, come back here. I can probably save you two or three hundred dollars."

He didn't look up again. I stood there several seconds, then left. About two months later I bought a new computer, monitor, scanner, and printer. I didn't buy them from the man in the shop. I'd have kept using my old equipment for another two years before I'd have gone back to him. Occasionally I pass his place and glance in. He always seems to be working, so I guess he hasn't suffered from the loss of my business. Still, it perplexes me that he passed up a reasonable chance of earning my three thousand bucks. I guess he thought it would be bad use of his time to chat with me for a few minutes. Maybe it would have, but I can't help thinking he'd have been none the worse if he had given me a friendly smile or offered me a chair. He could have said, "Tell me what your needs are and I'll recommend a system that you'll be happy with for years. And I think you'll be pleasantly surprised at how little it costs." If he had done something like that, he probably would have had me for a customer, maybe more than once.

Perhaps he has more work than he can handle. Maybe he is normally a charmer and snake oil salesman deluxe. But based on my encounter with him, I have to think that if he treated customers a bit more kindly, he could double or triple his business. I'm brash enough to think I could teach him how to do it, and I've never even been in sales. I'd like to have the opportunity to show him how much more enjoyment he could get from his business—how much more pleasant and rewarding it would be, how much easier it would be to attract customers. I'd like to show him how a word here and a smile there could open doors, draw people to him, even make them want to please him. Well, I suppose I'll never have that chance. Too bad.

TREATING PEOPLE AS YOU WOULD CUSTOMERS

Let's move our attention back to the classroom. We all want students to get along well together, for their sake and ours. One of the best ways to help is to teach them some of the human relations skills top salespersons use. Imagine what it would do for personal relations if all of us treated others as if they were potential customers upon whom our livelihood depended. Good salespersons welcome customers in a friendly manner and put them at ease. They make them feel appreciated. They do this by smiling, extending a pleasant greeting, and asking how they can be of help. Business owners (except for a few like the sullen old computer-man) want customers treated that way because it encourages them to buy. Even if no sale is made, the customer is left with an inviting impression that might bring him or her back later. Word gets around about good places to do business.

I once knew a woman who fancied a dilapidated ice cream store in a dingy corner just off the beach. For a long time she spoke of how she could take that little corner, spruce it up, and make a real popular business out of it. She said that the first thing she'd do is hire two employees who would smile happily at every person who came by the store. She said she'd fire them if she ever saw them fail to smile. I thought that lady had just the right spirit and attitude.

We educators are not in the sales business, at least not directly. We don't have to ask our potential clients (students) how we might help them. But we can't go wrong when we do, especially when we smile and greet them pleasantly and treat them with respect. If we all acted that way in the classroom it would be a pretty nice place to spend time. Basic simple concept, isn't it? We ought to teach the concept to students and practice it ourselves and never leave home without it.

Here's hoping you aren't put off by the clerk and customer stories. You may think if we carry that notion too far we'll turn students into insincere hucksters who exude fakery and flattery. Indeed there is a line of sincerity we must be mindful of, but when it comes to effective human relations, most of us err on the conservative side. We don't sin grievously when we wish somebody a good day or tell them how nice it has been to see them even when in our hearts we don't necessarily mean what we say. Those little white lies (when they are such) do no harm and usually sweeten human relations.

THE MEANING OF HUMAN RELATIONS

Human relations have to do with the ways we treat each other in a variety of situations. When we say "good" human relations, we mean dealing with each other in ways that all the participants find beneficial or satisfying. In the classroom, we are mainly concerned about how students treat each other—what Alberto and Reynald say and do to each other—and how teacher and students interact—how Mrs. Johnson treats Alberto, and he her. In these various encounters we can say and do certain things that help us get along better and other things that cause friction. What we hope to accomplish in the classroom is to keep relationships positive and productive. Books of etiquette can be of help, especially where good manners are concerned. It's not a bad idea for students to learn some etiquette. You might want to spend a bit of class time on it. But for the most part, teachers needn't become overly technical about the social graces. We just want to help students know how to attract the other person's attention, give them undivided attention in return, and leave the impression they are nice people with whom to associate and work. If we didn't care whether students cooperated with, bullied, or intimidated each other, we could forget about human relations. But we do care about those things, and about students' trusting each other and enjoying learning and otherwise having a satisfying time in school. We help ourselves and our students, in that regard, by giving attention to human relations. Doing so also paves the way to synergy. Let's see how that is done.

SPECIFIC THINGS WE TRY TO ACCOMPLISH

The following are important interrelational skills we hope to help students acquire for use in the classroom and elsewhere. You can discuss and practice these skills in class meetings where students feel safe and don't mind laughing about mistakes. A good skill to begin with is the ice-breaker protocol shown in Figure 8.1.

Break the Ice

It is difficult for many of us to begin interacting with others, especially strangers. The process needn't be difficult. All we need is a good way to break the ice and get started. This may sound a bit elementary, but you'd be surprised how much students benefit from some help on how to initiate conversation with people they don't know well. Do some of these in class. Students like them.

1. Smile and say hello.
2. Introduce yourself: "My name is..." Allow the other person to introduce himself or herself. Listen carefully to the name. Repeat it. Associate it with something you know well so you won't forget it. When in doubt, ask how the person spells it. Use it immediately.
3. Ask the other person something specific to the situation in which you find yourselves: "Alicia, how long do you suppose we'll have to wait for the bus to get here?"

Figure 8.1 Protocol for breaking the ice.

Make a Good First Impression

First impressions have a lot to do with how quickly we can begin interacting productively. Obviously, people are more inclined to have dealings with us when we make a good impression than when we don't. The steps listed in Figure 8.1—smile, introduce yourself, and learn and use the other person's name—are among the best ways of making a good first impression. A genuine smile attracts others, as does using their name. If we say something cordial or interesting, we become even more attractive. Soon we are being treated like an old chum.

Open up Communication

One of the great dividing characteristics among people is that some communicate with strangers at the drop of a hat while others find it awkward. Those who need help profit from using door openers and empathetic listening, both discussed in Chapter 4. The ice-breaker protocol is a good way to initiate conversation. As the other person responds, we can use door openers such as "Interesting. Tell me more about it." "What do you think we'd have to do if we tried something like that? Would it be possible?" "I've never worked on anything like this. How could we make it happen?" As they respond, listen carefully in order to grasp not only what they are saying but, also, what it means to them. Take mental notes. From time to time ask if you understand correctly.

Predispose the Other Person to Cooperate

At times you may find yourself in a work relationship with someone who for one reason or another is not inclined to cooperate. Let's say this happens with a new student named Dennis. The two of you are assigned to make an oral report on the moons of Saturn. From the ice-breaker conversation you get the idea that Dennis likes you well enough but is not going to do his part of the assignment. He says he has to work after school and doesn't have time to practice any speeches. He says he will write his part out and you or the teacher can read it. You listen to him carefully and get the impression that what is really bothering him is making the oral presentation, not doing the work. You say, "Dennis, I'm wondering if we can work out a deal. I'll make the report to the class if you'll help look up the information and get it in order. We could call you the consultant and me the reporter. It might be fun. Want to try it?"

Confer Dignity

One of the most powerful techniques we have for influencing other people is to confer dignity on them (Figure 8.2). We do this by making them feel valued and respected. We help them feel valued when we remember to use their name and mention something notable we have learned about them. We show our respect by treating them courteously as an equal human being, asking their opinion, listening to them, and acknowledging their contributions. This makes others more inclined to seek us out, ask our advice, and cooperate with us. In the process we receive a great bonus: Those upon whom we confer dignity give us the same in return. Many people never seem to understand that they cannot gain stature by gossiping and running others down. That actually causes others to be wary and mistrustful of you. The best way to gain stature is through conferring dignity. If someone asks you how you can best build a solid reputation, tell them the following: Be ethical, approach everyone with respect, and take note of their positive qualities.

Build Trust

Chapter 2 described how to build bonds of trust with students. There we explored seven ethical principles that teachers must continually exhibit if trust is to develop. Five of those principles—kindness, consideration, helpfulness, fairness, and honesty—should be emphasized in student work groups that need to build trusting relationships. Those five principles and how they are manifested in personal behavior should be discussed in classroom meetings and then consciously practiced during group interactions until the behaviors involved become established.

---

1. Pay attention to them.
2. Ask their opinion.
3. Listen to them empathetically. (Understand their words; read their body language; try to interpret how they feel about what they are saying.)
4. Follow up on what they say. (Mention it; act on it.)
5. Call attention to their contributions. (Give credit publicly for what they have contributed or taught.)

Figure 8.2 How to confer dignity on others.

HOW, SPECIFICALLY, DO WE BEHAVE IN GOOD HUMAN RELATIONS?

We have considered the nature of human relations skills, what we try to accomplish through their use, and principles to keep in mind when using them. But we have not focused on the specific behaviors we use in human relations that carry our messages to others. Here is what we try to do and how (students usually enjoy role-playing these behaviors):

Use Positive Body Language

The most powerful medium we have for conveying messages to others is body language, also called nonverbal communication. Body Language is the physical mannerisms we display when interacting. Notable are facial expression, eye contact, gestures, body posture, and proximity. Sometimes our body language supports what we are saying verbally. Sometimes it does not. When what we are saying with words seems different from what we are saying with our bodies, the physical message is the stronger of the two. Imagine that you are introduced to someone who says, "Delighted to meet you," but gives you an unenthusiastic handshake and looks away from you with a bored expression. Do you believe this person is really delighted? How about if the person looks you in the eye, smiles, gives you a warm handshake, and invites you to sit down? It's a different story then, isn't it?

The old saying about actions speaking louder than words holds true in all human interactions. Stephen R. Covey (1989) claims that on the average only 10 percent of our communication is conveyed by words, 30 percent by the sounds we make when speaking, and 60 percent by our body language. One might quibble with his figures, but he's right that we are more likely to understand what a person is really feeling or saying by interpreting speech sounds and body language than by relying verbatim on the spoken words.

Suppose we are discussing the topic of communication with our students. What advice can we give to help them improve? Students easily understand the importance of eye contact, facial expression, and body positioning, though they may never consciously think of them when communicating. Most western societies emphasize eye contact. This varies among groups within the larger society: If you encounter such differences, make appropriate adjustments. Most people consider a smile or a pleasant expression welcoming and receptive. Nodding while looking at the other indicates agreement or understanding. When you stand near another person and face them you are indicating receptiveness. When you maintain distance or turn to the side you send a message of rejection. That may not be what you intend. We can help students learn to match their body language to their intentions.

Send Clear Verbal Messages

We send verbal messages by two means—speaking and writing. Most people assume direct vocal communication is the most effective way to communicate, but this is not always so. Written communication may be more precise than spoken communication so far as the actual words are concerned. What it does not provide is body language and accompanying sounds that help us interpret more fully what the other person wants to communicate saying. Even if only 10 percent of our face-to-face communication is carried by words, we should not discount the impact of spoken messages. Words are very powerful. Not only do they allow us to convey what we intend, they have the power to instill hope, or mislead and hurt. We must use them judiciously.

Be Aware of How Our Words Sound

We saw the contention that 30 percent of the meaning we garner from what others say comes from the sounds they make when speaking, rather than from the literal meaning of their words. These sounds, such as intonation, inflection, and emphasis, modify the meanings of words. Compare the word "yes" when spoken flatly with "yes" spoken with a rising inflection. The first can be taken literally, but the second can convey various fuzzy meanings such as, "What do you want?" or "What are you up to now?" Intonation, inflection, and plays on words add spice to human interaction and are good for helping people relate positively. They can have negative effects too. We should alert our students to how intonation and plays on words affect the meanings of what we say to others. We should show them clearly how certain inflections and word emphases produce sarcasm.

React Positively to Others

Suppose someone is sharing information with us. We want to remain on good terms with them so we can continue working together productively. How should we react to what they say? Should we be entirely honest? If what they say sounds crazy to us, should we tell them so? Yes, we should, but not in so many words. Our response must be made tactfully. If our reaction is positive, fine. We can nod and show agreement. If uncertain, we can ask for more information, such as "Tell me more about that," or "You know, that idea is new to me. Could you explain it a bit further?" If we disagree with what they say, we should give our opinion gently. It is always good to say something like, "I may be wrong, but I see it a bit differently," and then give our view. "I may be wrong . . ." is one of the best ways to disagree with others. It doesn't put them on the defensive and they are usually ready to hear your opinion.

When we agree with what others say, and when we find them interesting, our body language is unequivocal. We turn toward them, look at them, nod, and remain alert. When we disagree, we tend to look away, purse our lips, and appear inattentive. These messages get across clearly. If we hope to collaborate with someone with whom we disagree, we must not alienate them. If we maintain good relations we have a chance of persuading them to our point of view. To make that possible, we can look at them, nod, and remain attentive even though we disagree with them. In that way we show interest in their views. At the same time, we can reply with "I may be wrong, but . . ." and then gently tell the other person what our position is.

Follow Through on Agreements

Students should know that we have to follow through on our agreements if we hope to maintain positive relationships. Suppose you are working with Jeff to plan a flyer announcing the upcoming science fair. From your previous conversation you know that Jeff would like to list the titles of the science exhibits and the names of the people involved in each. You feel the flyer will attract more attention with a futuristic theme and a high-quality illustration. At your last meeting each of you expressed your view and each agreed to contact at least five members of the community and ask them which of the two schemes they'd find more appealing. If you want to continue in Jeff's good graces, you'd better follow through with what you promised by obtaining the opinions and the reasons to support them. Jeff is not going to think much of you as a work partner if you appear with some excuse about why you couldn't do what you agreed to do (Figure 8.3).

```
1. Smile and greet others pleasantly.
2. Use positive body language.
3. Send clear verbal messages.
4. Be mindful of how our words sound.
5. React positively to what others say.
6. Follow through on agreements.
```

Figure 8.3 A summary of what we do to maintain good human relations.

What, Specifically, We Should Make Sure Not to Do

Just as there are specific things we try to do when interacting with others, so are there things we must make sure not to do (Figure 8.4). If we want to maintain good relations, we should never *slight* the other person, never give them less than our full attention and never give them less credit than they are due. It is much better to give them undeserved recognition and credit than show you do not appreciate their collaboration. There may indeed be times when you don't feel they've done their part or have not followed through, or are simply lazy and stubborn. You may think they are taking advantage of you and you might do well to tell them so. But if you do, focus only on the work done or not done; don't make remarks that are hurtful to them personally. If you do, you probably can never work productively with them again. That is a question you will have to think through.

Just as you never slight a coworker, neither do you ever *put them down*. You don't make disparaging comments about them. You don't call them inept, lazy, or stupid. You don't speak sarcastically and then laugh as if you didn't mean it. The message gets across loud and clear that you *did* mean it, exactly as you said. Fellow workers may occasionally forgive you for putting them down in private, provided you apologize sincerely, but they never forgive you for doing so in public. And they never, ever forget. Again, it may seem to you they deserve public disapproval. Maybe they have procrastinated, behaved foolishly, or failed to do their part. But you gain nothing by commenting on their failures. The best thing you can do under the circumstances is to carry out your role the best you can. If you get on their case, they will probably avoid working with you. Maybe that is what you want, but maybe it is not.

We also need to make sure we do not *discount out of hand* what our colleagues say or do. You destroy harmonious relations when you say something like, "Tomás thinks we should get the work done by tomorrow, but we believe he is out of touch. The rest of us agree it will take a minimum of three days." Imagine how it makes Tomás feel to have his views discounted in that manner. Neither do we want to *reply sarcastically* to what Tomás says. When he indicates he feels the work can be done by the next day, you certainly don't want to reply, "Tomorrow? Oh right. Sure. Where have you been hiding?" You produce the same effect by *snickering* or *rolling your eyes* when Tomás gives his opinion. These admonitions may seem common sense, yet we see students, teachers, and other adults do them all the time. You'd think they would know better, but all too often people still like to demonstrate their imagined superiority by putting others in their place. If Tomás says the work can be done by tomorrow, you'd do much better replying, "You think so? I may be wrong, but I estimated it would take me a couple of days to get my part done. I hope you are right. Maybe I miscalculated—I figured it would take me all of tomorrow to get the preliminary sketches done and then another full day to get them into final form."

---

1. We do not show disinterest in the other person.
2. We do not slight the other person.
3. We do not put down the other person.
4. We do not discount the other's contributions out of hand.
5. We do not speak sarcastically to, or of the other person.

Figure 8.4 A Summary of what we try not to do in human relations.

WHEN DO WE BEST LEARN AND PRACTICE HUMAN RELATIONS SKILLS?

Human relations skills are best introduced and first practiced in class meetings. They can then transfer to normal student interactions. The skills are not hard to teach. Students needn't fuss and fight their way through preadolescence or so often become angry and pout and cry. It should be noted that some authorities, including psychologist Jean Piaget (1951) and education critic Alfie Kohn (1996), contend that arguing and squabbling help students develop intellectually and socially. My view is that we can help them learn to get along without traumatizing themselves and everyone around them while doing so. The role that human relations plays in the ability to collaborate can hardly be overemphasized. The ability to get along and work together has become essential in today's workplace. Its potential for bettering relations within families is equally important.

Skills such as those we explore in this chapter can be isolated and introduced, then practiced through role-playing (Figure 8.4). We provide a safe venue while students learn what to say, how to say it, how to use body language, and how to maintain positive feelings during disagreements. Matters concerning what to do when human relations go sour can be discussed and strategies for correcting mistakes can be explored. From class meetings, the new skills can be carried over into actual work sessions. Later, students can discuss how well they were able to maintain a positive focus and can discuss points where they feel relationships were put under stress.

OPPORTUNE TIMES FOR IMPLEMENTING HUMAN RELATIONS SKILLS

Human relations are important in all our interactions with other people, but there are certain times when they are especially useful. The impressions we make when we *first meet someone* can be strongly positive, somewhat negative, or eminently forgettable. Not long ago I attended a preview of a large art exhibition. Certain people, for one reason or another, were invited to the exhibition hall a day ahead of the general public. That gave us an opportunity to talk with some of the artists as well as community patrons. I met one gentleman who learned I was an educator and writer. He memorized my name and used it three or four times in the next few minutes. He asked what I thought of the exhibit and whether I agreed with the judges' awards. He even offered me a drink. Now that fellow, I'd be glad to see him any time, discuss matters with him, work with him. There were some others I met, too, including a couple of artists, who were memorable.

Others made less of an impression (I probably affected them the same way). One lady so epitomized what we *shouldn't* do in human relations I think I'll remember her for a long time. She didn't look at me when we were introduced. She looked off to the side while speaking the two or three sentences she managed and I didn't understand anything she said. She looked as though she'd rather be anywhere than in the exhibition hall meeting a stranger. Somehow I didn't come away with the feeling I could collaborate very well with her. Of course, those were only first impressions and might not have represented her accurately. But I'll probably never see the lady again and will therefore always have that memory of her.

The interest we communicate when *greeting* another person, including persons we have known for a long time, affects the potential for interaction. When we are happy to see someone we usually show it through excitement and tone of voice. When preoccupied, we may appear less enthusiastic, causing the other person to feel we are not overly pleased to see them. The same can be said for how we *make our departure* from a meeting with others. When we say how good it was to see them and really seem to mean it, it makes the other person think well of us and look forward to seeing us again. If we slight them or appear unenthusiastic they are more likely to think, "Who needs this bozo?" and immediately mark us off the guest list for their next dinner party. The interactions we have during *daily living* are golden times for improving our relationships with people in our lives.

My significant other has commented on occasion (always lovingly) that I am at times less than fully communicative. At first this came as a surprise, for I could hear a stream of talk going on inside my head most of the time. Sometimes it was related to what she was talking about and sometimes not, but I never realized I was a complete dud at the breakfast table. Once I thought about what she said I realized of course she was right, as always. I try to remember her advice in social gatherings where small talk is golden. I do better in work settings where we vie to hit the target with our lance-like wit, and family evenings at the knee of the television where we poke fun at stupid dialog and idiotic plots. (We feel it is all right to slight people and call them names when we restrict it to television characters, but we never do that to real people.) Oh, and I have learned not to talk about people behind their backs. I appreciate it when an author teaches me something important, as Stephen R. Covey did in his book *The Seven Habits of Highly Effective People* (1989). In particular I liked what he said concerning how we should speak of people who are not present. He was writing of integrity and its essential role in good human relations. He said,

> One of the most important ways to manifest integrity is to *be loyal to those who are not present*. When you defend those who are absent, you retain the trust of those present. (p. 196)

WHAT ABOUT HUMAN RELATIONS IN THE PRIMARY GRADES?

Most of the illustrations provided in this chapter refer to students who are able to do logical reasoning. Generally speaking, they are nine years old or more. You may be wondering what we can teach younger children about human relations. The answer is: practically everything we've covered. There is no problem in that regard. Little children understand the Golden Rule, taking turns, being nice to others, and getting along without fussing or fighting. Naturally they can't discuss human relations in the depth that older students can, but they have no trouble learning the basic premises. The teacher must introduce and guide the discussion. Two examples of how primary teachers approach this important matter follow.

Ruth's Kindergarten

Teaching human relations at the early primary level is not just a matter for teacher and students but involves parents as well. A key aspect is modelling proper behavior. Young children learn by imitating the behavior of adults in their lives. Unfortunately, adults don't always demonstrate desirable behavior. One parent told me, "I am glad I like the way you act, because Jenny tries to act just like you."

School principals can set excellent examples for young children. The two most recent principals at my school have stood on the steps in the morning to greet parents, teachers, and students as they arrive. Everybody likes this. It helps students learn to greet others with a smile and a cheery good morning. Children have said to me about the principal, "I like him; he knows my name."

The importance of human relations with parents cannot be stressed enough. The relationship between parent and teacher has a great influence on how effective the teacher is with the child. That means we teachers have to cultivate the good will of parents. I always try to follow the Golden Rule with parents just as with children. Basically, this is what I try to do with children:

1. Talk about how we feel when others push, call us names, or don't play with us.
2. Discuss treating others as we like to be treated. Remind students of this every day.
3. Always be honest and respectful when speaking with children.
4. Always treat every child with dignity. Don't embarrass them in front of others.
5. Choose words carefully. Don't accuse them of doing something wrong; that only makes them defensive. Don't ask them, "Did you . . . ?" or "Why did you . . . ?" Just politely ask, "What could you have done differently?"
6. When two students disagree, find a way to let both of them feel satisfied.

When I am working with parents, here is what I try to do:

1. Choose my words carefully when telling the parent of their child's misbehavior or inadequate performance. I never accuse the child or make the parent feel the situation is their fault. I remember that they see the child as an extension of themselves. Parents will not cooperate with me if I attack or blame their child. The approach I take is suggesting what the parent and I together can do to help the child be more successful.
2. I try to convince the parent that I want the same for their child that they do: a successful school experience.

Some teachers exhibit good human relations skills and others do not. The most successful teachers I know practice them assiduously.

Cynthia's Second-Grade Class

I begin the year with a discussion about my expectations for the year. I tell the children that I consider them my school family. I explain that just as in any family we might not always agree on everything, nonetheless I will always care about them. I say that each and every one of them is very special and important to me and that I want them to have the best possible school year.

Because they are so important to me, we cannot allow any cruelty or unkindness to each other. I expect them to be the best behaved and well-mannered class in the entire school, both in the classroom and on the playground. I tell them that good behavior is really just good manners, because it shows respect for others, whether children or adults. I also go over the Golden Rule, and I make a bulletin board on that theme. I refer to the Golden Rule as our class motto. That is the only rule we have in the class, and I discuss with them how it covers everything, such as: If you don't want to be called names, then don't call other people names. If you want people to listen to you, then be sure to listen to others. And most important, if you want to have friends, then be a friend.

The children seem to understand and accept all of this very well. They see it as a fair and sensible way to do things, and I think it helps them know they have a teacher who cares about them.

I have very much liked what Cynthia tells her children: *Good behavior is just good manners in which you show respect for others.*

WHERE DO WE GO FROM HERE?

We have completed examination of the eighth of the nine elements that combine to produce class synergy. In this chapter we have seen that good human relations increase the potential for effective collaboration with others, which makes more likely the release of energy that leads to classroom synergy. We move now to a consideration of problem resolution, the ninth and final element needed for synergy. Problems and conflicts are inevitable when groups of people are placed in a confined space and asked to work together. We will see how those problems can be resolved so that positive attitudes and good personal relations are maintained.

To Think About

1. Recall an instance when you agreed to collaborate with another person or group of people in an educational or community endeavor, but found a strong difference of opinion within the group. What happened concerning human relations in that effort? Did things go smoothly or was there conflict? In terms of what you read in this chapter, what might have been done to improve the process?

2. We know it is quite common for group members to squabble among themselves. Do you feel the process can be smoothed and improved through elimination of "fighting words," or do you feel that hotly stated opinions are needed in resolving group disagreements?

3. Suppose you decide to make an effort to improve human relations within your class. What specifically would you focus on? How much time would you spend on it? Would you use classroom meetings as the venue for learning and practicing skills? Would you use role-playing? Can you see dangers in role-playing negative responses such as sarcasm and name-calling?

4. Suppose in your class you have worked hard on good human relations. Your students have responded well and personal relations in the class are good. What might you do to encourage students to use the skills in interactions with others such as family and friends outside the class?

RESOLVING NONDISCIPLINARY PROBLEMS AND CONFLICTS

Shawn, I think I've finally pinpointed the cause of your misbehavior: You feel hopeless, unaccepted, powerless, bored, and incompetent. Am I right?

THE DAY I FLUNKED PROBLEM-SOLVING

When I was teaching school, the students treated me pretty well. They were friendly and usually appreciative of what I tried to do for them. Occasionally, however, incidents happened that, while humorous now, were anything but funny then. One instance that has remained fresh in my mind occurred in my second year of teaching. It was a high school Spanish class. I got along well with the students and they held no animosity toward me so far as I knew. Each class session began with a regular assignment, which was to read a paragraph in Spanish and decide what it meant in English. I would sit in a chair, check attendance, and fill out the attendance report while they read. After a few minutes we would discuss the meaning of the paragraph, give attention to idiomatic expressions and sentence organization, and practice speaking the phrases. One morning I came in, asked the class to begin reading, and sat down in my chair. Immediate shock. I had sat in a puddle of cold water that soaked the back of my trousers. I jumped up. The wide eyes of every student were fixed on me. Their faces were expressionless. I tipped the remaining water out of the chair and said, "I'll be back as soon as I can." I walked out, dripping. I hurried to the office and asked one of the secretaries to keep an eye on the class. I lived not far from school, so I dashed home and changed pants. I was back in less than 30 minutes. When I returned, I proceeded with the lesson as if nothing had happened. (This was probably the best way to handle the situation, but I did it by accident.) At the end of the period the students left the room. All eyes were averted. No one spoke to me or to each other. There was definitely a problem and I owned it, but I didn't know what to do. As days went by, some of the students from the class sidled up to me and whispered they hadn't had anything to do with what happened in the class. I never knew who was responsible nor why they did it. Perhaps someone was upset with me, or maybe they were caught up in a prank or dare. I never tried to find out. As you can see, I was a real whiz at problem-solving in those days.

TEACHING, PROBLEMS, AND CONFLICTS

Teaching brings a steady stream of problems, most of which must be resolved quickly if learning is to occur as intended. Materials are lost, homework is not completed, unexpected visitors appear, students disrupt, fight, show lack of respect, and sometimes lie, steal, and cheat. They may even put water in your chair. For a few fortunate teachers, these problems don't appear often and only occasionally does one reach major proportions. For an unfortunate few, problems come in a steady stream and are sometimes serious.

Success in teaching, or lack thereof, is largely determined by how effectively teachers resolve problems and conflicts. When difficulties appear, teachers have three options: One is to ignore the situation, as I did when I got waterlogged. At times, if the problem is not serious, that's the best approach, but if there is danger of escalation, you've got to intervene. A second option is to decide on a solution unilaterally and simply tell students what to do. That was the old-fashioned way of resolving problems, one I considered when standing there in wet pants. A great many teachers still try to use that approach, but it hasn't brought much success since students began to resist being ordered about. A third option for dealing with problem situations is to involve students meaningfully in their resolution. We have seen that students are more cooperative when they have a hand in making decisions and are more likely to support teachers who grant them this responsibility. That is what I should have done with my Spanish students. I would have if I'd had any notion about how to proceed, but alas! I'm afraid I flunked problem resolution that morning.

But what are problems? What causes one situation to be called a problem while another is just an occurrence? How do we solve problems? Do problems call for disciplinary tactics? What about conflicts? Are they the same as problems?

When we use the word **problem,** we are usually referring to a situation that affects the class seriously enough to require remediation. It may have slowed class work, made work more difficult, or had a detrimental effect on class members' feelings. Problems do not necessarily involve clashes of will. Many do not involve misbehavior. We refer to problems with no conflict or misbehavior as *nondisciplinary* and approach them differently than we do problems that involve misbehavior.

Conflicts, on the other hand, are strong disputes between students or between student and teacher. They involve contests of will. One side is pitted against another, with neither willing to back down. They may involve misbehavior and if so are resolved through disciplinary tactics described in Chapter 10. If they do not involve misbehavior, they are approached through win/win conflict resolution, described in this chapter.

Our present task is to explore the resolution of nondisciplinary problems and conflicts. We begin with problems, which we approach through the following scenarios.

FOUR SCENARIOS

Scenario #1. Mr. Crane Has a Messy Classroom.

Mr. Crane teaches a class of lively second-grade students. He keeps things interesting for them and they respond with enthusiasm, at times exuberance. They read from their reading books and act out the roles of characters. They make props for their skits. They do sets of practice activities in mathematics every morning. Mr. Crane, a good artist, provides pencil and paper drawing activities and painting at easels. The class is happy and so is Mr. Crane, although recently one thing has begun to bother him: The classroom is disheveled most of the time. Papers are strewn about the floor. Books are tumbled on the shelves. The area around the easels is spattered with paint. Student desks are cluttered. Mr. Crane didn't worry about this untidiness until his principal began a series of lesson evaluations and commented on the lack of neatness in the room. She said it encouraged students to be untidy and was unfair to the custodian because it left him so much cleaning to do. The principal wrote on Mr. Crane's evaluation that improvement was needed in materials management and neatness. Mr. Crane wanted a good evaluation so he suddenly became concerned about the room's appearance. He told the students they were going to have to be neater. They tried for a day or two but soon the room looked as it did before. Mr. Crane began spending lots of time walking about picking up scraps of paper, straightening books, and scrubbing up spots and spills. He talked to the students again and asked them if they couldn't do a better job of helping. Once more they tried but soon lapsed into their old habits. One day Mr. Crane became so exasperated he made them stay in during afternoon recess to put the room in order. This upset the students who muttered about its being unfair. Mr. Crane sensed tension in the class that was not there before. When the time for his next evaluation arrived, he crossed his fingers and hoped to heaven the students would remember to keep the room neat.

Questions about Mr. Crane's messy classroom:

1. Is there a genuine problem here?
2. For whom does the problem exist? How can we tell?
3. Is it a discipline problem?
4. If there is a problem, how should it be brought up and considered?
5. If there is a problem, how can it best be resolved?
6. If a solution is found, how can it be codified?

Let's think about these questions a bit.

What constitutes a problem?(Figure 9.1) My old friend Professor Elmer D. Baldwin taught me long ago that something is a problem when it is perceived as such. If nobody considers it a problem, then it's not. This realization startled me at first. I had grown up thinking certain things were problems by dint of their nature (e.g., famine, crime) while others (e.g., wealth, lots of new clothes) were not. Elmer pointed out that having a lot of money can sometimes be a problem, and lack of new clothing is often not a problem at all. It all depends on the point of view of those involved. Thomas Gordon (1989), somewhat more famous than Elmer Baldwin, says something similar. Gordon believes problem resolution requires determining what constitutes a problem and who owns it. (He says whoever is affected adversely by the problem "owns" it.) Like Elmer Baldwin, Gordon says you have a problem if you believe you do, but otherwise you don't. Gordon goes so far as to say that students do not think of their behavior as a problem. He says misbehavior is an adult concept that bothers teachers but not students. I can't go along fully with that view because I think students have concepts of misbehavior, too, and are often troubled by the way other students behave.

Let's go back to the first question: Is there a genuine problem with the messy classroom? Yes, there is because someone sees it as a problem. In this case, the principal has identified it as a condition that needs correcting. It bothers her. Her judgment, in turn, has caused Mr. Crane to see it as a problem, though he didn't originally. It is now a problem for him because it causes him to worry about getting a good evaluation.

Is it a discipline problem in Mr. Crane's room? Once a problem is identified, we can determine whether it is a nondisciplinary problem or a discipline problem. It is judged to be a **discipline problem** if, first, the situation involves *intentional student misbehavior* and, second, if it is

> A situation is considered to be a problem if someone is unduly troubled by it. In the classroom, teachers are likely to feel unduly troubled by situations that:
> 1. Interfere more than casually with classwork and progress.
> 2. Have a detrimental effect on the feelings of the teacher and/or students.
> 3. Have a strong potential for impeding work or damaging feelings.

Figure 9.1 What constitutes a problem.

troubling to someone (Figure 9.2). From that definition, we can see that the messy classroom is not a discipline problem–it does not involve willful student misbehavior, that is, behavior done intentionally even when the student knows it is disapproved. It does trouble Mr. Crane, but not because it interferes with teaching or learning.

The distinction between discipline problems and nondisciplinary problems is important because the two are resolved differently. Nondisciplinary problems ordinarily involve no conflict between teacher and student. Discipline problems on the other hand are characterized by a clash of wills, teacher against students. Teachers almost always win those contests, in the short run, and almost always lose them in the long run. The teacher gets his or her way, but in the process loses student trust and cooperation. Negative emotions remain in the "loser" long after the confrontation is over.

If there is a problem, how should it be brought up and considered? If the problem is hindering teaching or learning, or if it causes feelings to run high, it should be addressed immediately. In the old approach, the teacher identified the problem and told the class what to do to correct it. The teacher might allow some discussion but essentially laid down the law which students had to follow. The more enlightened teacher senses the problem and simply says, "Class, something troublesome is going on that I think we need to talk about now. Let's move our chairs into a circle." If the problem is not hindering teaching or learning and if feelings have not become inflamed, the matter can be brought up at a more convenient time, such as at a scheduled class meeting. The topic can be introduced by teacher or student. A high school class might complain about heavy loads of homework that impinge on weekend activities, and a class discussion can bring out the nature of the problem as students see it. Or a teacher such as Mr. Crane might say, "Class, when the principal visited, she said our room seemed too messy. She wants us to keep it neater. What do you think—have you noticed the mess? How can we keep the room nice and neat?" In both cases the class is clarifying the problem, which is step #1 shown in Figure 9.3

> A problem is considered to be a discipline problem if it:
> Involves *intentional violation* of class agreements and causes somebody to feel upset.

Figure 9.2 What constitutes a discipline problem.

1. Clarify the problem. Try to state exactly what is occurring and why it is a problem.
2. Discuss possible solutions. Use brainstorming. Listen to everyone's ideas.
3. From the suggested solutions, select one or more likely that seem to produce the desired results. List them on the board or a chart.
4. Try the proposed solution. See how it works in practice. Modify it if necessary.

Figure 9.3   Suggested procedure for resolving nondisciplinary problems.

If there is a problem, how can it best be resolved? The class clarifies the problem and proceeds with the remaining steps until a proposed solution is selected. It takes time to involve the class in this manner, considerably more than when the teacher just tells them what to do, but we have noted that directives do not promote class cooperation. For a good result, the class needs to buy into the solution. They are much more likely to do so if they propose it. If it's their idea, they want it to be successful and they like knowing they have a say in making the decisions.

Thomas Gordon advises teachers to envision a "behavior window," a graphic concept that helps identify who owns the problem and what ought to be done about it. Figure 9.4 illustrates Gordon's suggestions.

Gordon says that by knowing who owns problems, the teacher is better able to take more appropriate action. He lists three categories of beneficial action the teacher can take:

1. *Confrontive skills* address the problem directly by modifying the environment, using I-messages that do not set off defensive mechanisms, and using effective methods of problem resolution. Mrs. Samuelsen uses a confrontive I-message when she tells the class how she feels about a situation, as a means of causing students to change their behavior, such as, "I am feeling uncomfortable about the noise in the room." Confrontive skills are employed when the teacher owns the problem.

Behavior Window	**Acceptability to Teacher**
The situation causes substantial worry for the student only. **Student owns the problem.**	The situation is acceptable to the teacher. Supportive action can be taken to help the student with the problem.
The situation causes no substantial worry for either students or teacher. **No problem.**	The situation is acceptable to the teacher. Preventive action can be taken to help the class keep problem situations to a minimum.
The situation causes substantial worry for the teacher. **Teacher owns the problem.**	The situation is unacceptable to the teacher. Confrontive action will be taken in an attempt to resolve the problem.

Figure 9.4   Problem ownership and suggested responses.
Source: Adapted from P.E.T. in Action (pp. 27, 174, 251) by T. Gordon, 1976. New York: Random House.

2. *Supportive skills* encourage students to solve problems with which they might be struggling. Mr. Martin uses supportive skills when he acknowledges students' concern and follows with active listening. He might say "I can see this lesson is not very interesting to you. Do you have any suggestions for making it better?" Supportive skills are used when the student owns the problem.

3. *Preventive skills* help keep potential problems from materializing. They include I-messages, problem-solving, and decision making. Miss Amable uses a preventive I-message when she refers to herself in a way that influences students' future behavior, such as, "We are going to walk together three blocks to the ice cream store for our treats. I need to make sure we all stay together so we won't have any problems." Preventive skills are used when no one owns the problem. They help minimize potential problems.

If a solution is found, how can it be codified? To codify the solution is to put it into a form that gives it ongoing power. You can do this through verbal agreement or by writing out the agreement and posting it. If you have a class code, you can add the agreement to it. In Mr. Crane's case, suppose the class has decided that they will resolve the problem by making each student responsible for keeping his or her desk and the surrounding area neat and tidy. That agreement needn't be written. It is sufficient for Mr. Crane to give verbal reminders occasionally or ask the class if they remember the agreement.

Scenario #2. Mr. Muller's First-Graders Are Slow to Enter the Room and Settle Down

Mr. Muller teaches a class of first-grade students. They are from various ethnic groups and almost half speak only rudimentary English. They are nice children, reasonably attentive and well-mannered, but are slow getting inside the room and into their seats. They mill around, talk, dawdle, and play with their lunch boxes and toys they have brought for sharing. This is especially noticeable first thing in the morning, but also occurs when the students come in from recess, lunch, and assemblies. Three to six minutes are lost on every occasion, wasting 15 to 20 minutes of instructional time each day. Mr. Muller has talked with the students about the need to enter quickly and get settled. They seem to understand at the time but soon forget. He has begun to scold them, which leaves them disconcerted and him feeling inept.

Exercise: Try answering the following questions about Mr. Muller's situation.

1. Is there a genuine problem here?
2. For whom does the problem exist? How can we tell?
3. Is it a discipline problem?
4. If there is a problem, how should it be brought up and considered?

Scenario #3. Profanity Abounds in Miss Wellborn's Sixth-Grade Class

Miss Wellborn teaches a sixth-grade class of gifted and talented students. They are lively and try to outdo each other in all matters. Recently they have begun using profanity in the classroom to a degree that alarms Miss Wellborn. She is no prude, but does not consider profanity appropriate in school. When she mentioned her concern to the class, the students said their parents speak that way and so does everybody in movies and television. They assure her it is the way kids talk nowadays and there is nothing wrong with it. They say, however, that they will tone the language down because they do not want to upset Miss Wellborn. Their actions do not match their assurances. Miss Wellborn feels the students are vying to see who can speak in the most outrageous manner. She doesn't like the fact that they laugh so much after making truly crude comments. She knows her students use profanity on the playground in earshot of other students and teachers and sometimes parents. In the back of her mind she expects the principal to speak to her about the students' language.

Exercise: Try answering the following questions about Miss Wellborn's predicament.

1. Is there a genuine problem here?
2. For whom does the problem exist? How can we tell?
3. Is it a discipline problem?
4. If there is a problem, how should it be brought up and considered?

Scenario #4. Jonathan Is Being Scapegoated in Geometry Class

Fritz Redl and William Wattenberg (1959) in their early studies of group behavior noted cases where students scapegoated particular members of the class—that is, students placed blame for misdeeds on a particular student even though they knew the student wasn't involved. They thought it fun to do so and it allowed them to pull mild shenanigans without being called to task. Not infrequently, scapegoated students accept their fate smilingly. Redl and Wattenberg interpreted this acquiescence as a mechanism insecure students use to gain approval from the group. This has been happening in Mr. Sipes's geometry class. Student Jonathan, overweight, unkempt, and phlegmatic, regularly gets fingers pointed at him for making noises, emitting odors, losing materials, and causing others to speak out in class when they shouldn't. Jonathan, though innocent of most of the accusations, smilingly accepts the blame. Sometimes when students accuse him of a transgression, he jokingly says, "Oh yeah, you too." Mr. Sipes suspects that Jonathan is being made a dupe of the class but is not sure. On one occasion, Jonathan was blamed for spilling two boxes of attribute blocks that clattered about on the floor. The class laughed for several minutes, further arousing Mr. Sipes's suspicions. Later, Mr. Sipes took Jonathan aside and asked if he had really spilled the blocks or if someone else had caused the spill. Jonathan looked away and said, "Yes, Sir. I did. I'm sorry." Mr. Sipes didn't believe Jonathan's admission but didn't know what else to say.

Exercise: Try answering our list of questions applied to Mr. Sipes's class.

1. Is there a genuine problem here?
2. For whom does the problem exist? How can we tell?
3. Is it a discipline problem?
4. If there is a problem, how should it be brought up and considered?

PROBLEMS AND THEIR RESOLUTION

We saw earlier that nondisciplinary problems are situations that involve no clash of wills but are nevertheless troublesome to teacher or students. They may interfere with class work and progress, have a detrimental effect on teachers' or students' feelings, or have a clear potential for impeding work or damaging feelings. In nondisciplinary problems there is only an obstacle to overcome. Neither teacher dignity nor student dignity is threatened. There is uncertainty about how to resolve the problem, but the situation does not stir up strong emotion. Examples of nondisciplinary problems (depending on the circumstances) might be: visitors interrupting lessons, uncomfortable lighting or heating, chronic tardiness, students not completing homework; materials being defaced or destroyed; failure to begin working expeditiously; not having materials students need for lessons; difficulty working together; and (depending on the circumstance) lying, stealing, and cheating.

In Figure 9.3 we saw that nondisciplinary problems are resolved as teacher and students work together to clarify the problem, brainstorm possible solutions, select and apply one or more promising solutions, and try out the solution in practice. When teacher and students become aware of a nondisciplinary problem, they often act together. Both may want to see it resolved and they work amicably toward a solution.

CONFLICTS AND THEIR RESOLUTION

Conflicts are problem situations that involve strong disagreements. Conflicts may or may not involve misbehavior. Here we will limit attention to nondisciplinary conflicts, those that do not involve misbehavior. In Chapter 10 we will see how conflicts involving misbehavior are resolved in the synergetic classroom.

Unlike problems, conflicts threaten the individuals involved. Both sides show emotion and put up protection against loss of dignity. Those involved in the conflict do not know how to work together to find a solution unless they have been trained to do so. Instead they fight each other verbally to prove they are in the right. Situations involving nondisciplinary conflict might include: who is or should be first in line; who won a contest; whether a player is safe or out; who is entitled to play with the toy; whether work was turned in on time; whether work was completed as assigned; and whether work met the standards expected.

Conflicts are resolved differently than problems (Figure 9.5). In problems, everyone pulls together toward a solution suitable to all. In nondisciplinary conflict resolution we try to find a solution that helps both sides feel they have "won," that is, have gotten more or less what they wanted. The procedure by which this is done is commonly called **win/win conflict resolution** (Figure 9.6). In the absence of win/win resolution, conflicts end up with one side "winning" and the other side "losing." For example, Ms. Allison and student Jerry have an emotional disagreement over the grade Jerry received on his theme. Jerry, highly motivated to receive good grades, complains. Ms. Allison justifies the grade and doesn't change it. In this case, Ms. Allison "wins" and Jerry "loses." That is the end of the matter, except that Jerry now harbors resentment against Ms. Allison.

In win/win conflict resolution, both sides emerge feeling they have won their point. There is no loser in the conflict. Let's go back to Ms. Allison and Jerry. The enlightened Ms. Allison listens to Jerry's complaint. She follows by explaining why she assigned the grade. Jerry still feels he has been wronged. Ms. Allison now asks, "I wonder what we might do so I can maintain my standards and you can receive the grade you want? Do you have any suggestions?" She and Jerry discuss options. They settle on a solution in which Jerry agrees to rewrite the theme, strengthening the weaknesses Ms. Allison identified in his work. In this way, both sides feel they are getting what they want. Jerry wants a good grade. Ms. Allison wants good work from Jerry that meets her standards. Neither feels they have lost the conflict.

The win/win process was first brought to wide attention by Thomas Gordon in his 1970 book *Parent Effectiveness Training*. There Gordon showed parents how to find common ground in disputes with their children so positive relationships could be maintained. He called the process "no-lose conflict resolution." Over the years, most authorities have come to call the process win/win, which has a more positive tone. It is now taught by leaders in education, business, counseling, and other

---

1. The situation involves a clash of wills between student and student or between teacher and student.
2. Emotions run high.
3. The people in dispute are inclined to attack the other verbally.
4. Each person puts up defenses against having their dignity damaged.

Figure 9.5   Characteristics of conflict.

fields. The advantage of win/win resolution as we saw for Ms. Allison and Jerry is threefold: (1) Damage to personal egos is minimized, thus preserving positive working relationships; (2) Motivation is maintained: those involved don't sulk or withdraw but continue working productively; and (3) Students learn a process they can use to reach satisfactory conclusions in other conflicts.

Here is a scenerio involving a strong conflict between student Martin and band director Mr. Weisskopf. See if you feel the win/win process could be used to resolve the conflict satisfactorily.

Conflict Scenario: Martin Verbally Attacks the Band Director

Martin holds first chair in the trombone section of the high school band. He is a talented player, but Mr. Weisskopf, the band director, feels Martin is slighting his talent. He is certain Martin doesn't practice sufficiently at home. Highly strung and short on patience, Mr. Weisskopf becomes exasperated when Martin makes routine errors in rehearsal and doesn't seem to give his best effort. One afternoon the band was practicing *Colonel Bogey*, a march with a strong brass line. Mr. Weisskopf selected the number in order to showcase Martin's talents in the upcoming concert. Even though the band had already practiced the number, Martin got the timing confused and didn't muster the volume that Mr. Weisskopf desired. After Martin made the mistake a second time, Mr. Weisskopf couldn't contain himself. He stared at Martin until the hall was very quiet, then said, "Sir, you are not practicing. You have talent, which makes it worse. Talent is nothing without effort and self-discipline. You are letting your ability go to waste. You are letting us all down with your laziness."

Martin, having a short fuse himself, retorted, "Don't single me out! I'm not the only one playing this part! How do you know how much I practice? You are a slave driver! Nobody ever pleases you no matter how hard they try!"

Mr. Weisskopf's face flamed. "You'll not speak to me in that manner!" he commanded.

"You can go to hell!" Martin shot back. He put his trombone in the case and left the room, jaws clenched.

Exercise: Initiating a resolution to the conflict is Mr. Weisskopf's duty. Suppose you are in his place. Would you try to resolve the dispute? If so, how? Could you use the win/win approach?

---

1. Key issues and the concerns of both disputants are identified and explained.
2. Each disputant tries genuinely to see the situation from the other's point of view.
3. Through discussion, the disputants identify solutions that seem acceptable to both.
4. The solution is implemented.

Figure 9.6 The win/win process of conflict resolution.

DEFUSING CONFRONTATIONS

You can see that the confrontation between Martin and Mr. Weisskopf should never have reached such proportions. Even when both disputants are volatile, such a result is inexcusable. It is the teacher's responsibility, by dint of position and understanding of conflict resolution, to defuse such situations before emotions become so inflamed neither side can listen or compromise.

Linda Albert (1996) provides good advice concerning how teachers should proceed when they are involved in a conflict or when they are mediating a conflict between students:

1. *Keep focus on the behavior, not the other person.* In the conflict between Jerry and Ms. Allison over the grade assigned to Jerry's theme, Ms. Allison was wise to focus on the theme, not Jerry. She did not blame him for the quality of his work. She simply pointed out areas that could be made stronger. In the conflict between band director Weisskopf and trombonist Martin, Mr. Weisskopf made a serious mistake in calling Martin lazy and undisciplined. (It doesn't matter whether Mr. Weisskopf was correct in his assessment—we are concerned only with resolving the conflict and keeping relationships open.) The result was that both Mr. Weisskopf and Martin put up defenses and said things that assaulted the other's dignity. That makes it difficult to reestablish positive cooperation between the two.

2. *Deal with the moment.* Keep the discussion focused on the matter at hand right now. Don't bring up what Jerry or Martin might have done in the past.

3. *Take charge of your negative emotions.* If you are involved in a conflict, it is very possible that your feelings will get hurt and you will become angry and combative, as Mr. Weisskopf did. You must not let that happen. You can't control the student's emotions, but you can control your own. Respond calmly and objectively. Don't raise your voice or wag your finger. Don't insist on the last word. When you behave in this manner you soften the student's desire to fight. If you are too emotional to retain self-control, tell the student you are not able to discuss the matter calmly but will do so later. Set an appointment for doing so and follow through.

4. *Allow students to save face.* Students know teachers have greater power than they do, so if there is a strong clash of wills they usually capitulate after venting their emotions. Instead of trying to make students knuckle under, calmly tell them you understand their concern and that you want to resolve it to everyone's satisfaction. Assure them of your desire to help them learn and feel successful. Ask them if they have suggestions about how to resolve the situation at hand and how such situations might be avoided in the future. This approach will usually calm students. Once the situation is resolved, follow up with friendly words and occasional chats.

TEACHING THE WIN/WIN RESOLUTION PROCESS TO STUDENTS

At a class meeting, bring up the topic of conflicts. Mention examples of conflicts that might arise in class or on the grounds. Explain the damaging results of resolutions that produce a winner and a loser. Introduce a strategy to help students deal with personal conflicts in which they might become involved. Jane Nelson, Lynn Lott, and H. Stephen Glenn (1997) suggest teaching students four tactics for resolving conflicts, as shown in Figure 9.7

Nelsen, Lott, and Glenn explain the four tactics as follows: Tactic 1 encourages students to step aside from the conflict or leave the area for a cooling-off period. The problem may resolve itself but might also fester to greater intensity. Tactic 2 allows students to tell each other what their concerns are and how they feel about them. Each listens attentively and respectfully to what the other says. Tactic 3 involves brainstorming possible solutions and then examining them to find one that might satisfy the concerns of both people. Tactic 4 asks for help from others when the conflict cannot be resolved by the people involved. Nelsen, Lott, and Glenn suggest displaying a chart of the four tactics. When students get involved in conflicts, point to the chart and ask them if they have tried any of the tactics. If they haven't, ask them which they would like to try. This prevents the teacher's being caught in a perpetual fix-it role.

Students encouraged to use win/win conflict resolution on their own will need your guidance and a good deal of practice. In class meetings where you discuss conflict and win/win resolution, give them scenarios to role play. Have them pretend to be angry and then substitute positive words and voices for angry ones. Have them listen attentively to the other person's point of view.

HOW TO TALK WITH PEOPLE WHO PRESENT A PROBLEM FOR YOU

It is difficult for most of us to talk persuasively with people we find authoritarian, verbose, hostile, or loud-spoken, or with people who hold positions of authority greater than ours. It is difficult for a timid student

---

1. Ignore the situation.
2. Talk the situation over respectfully with the other student.
3. Find a win/win solution.
4. If no solution can be found, put the item on the class meeting agenda for the class to discuss.

Figure 9.7 Four tactics for students to consider in resolving conflicts with others.

to talk with the class bully, and for teachers to talk on an equal footing with school administrators. Yet win/win conflict resolution depends on our being able to do so. To be successful we must function on the same level as the person with whom we are disputing. Here are some suggestions for win/win resolution. If you have time, make a copy of the suggestions and show them to the other person. Discuss the suggestions and ask the other person if her or she feels they can talk with you in the ways indicated.

1. *Make sure each person has a chance to talk.* Each should listen to the other carefully without resisting, defending oneself, or debating.
2. *All ideas should be presented in a friendly way.* This is not a contest. The objective is to find a good solution.
3. *Be honest and open.* Both should agree that if they are wrong about something, they will admit it. Doing so reduces defensiveness.
4. *Each person should try honestly to see things from the other's perspective.* Show respect for the other's opinions. Be sympathetic with his or her ideas and desires. Never say the other person is wrong; he or she might be right. Carefully note points of agreement.
5. *Each person should focus on areas of agreement.* Both should avoid saying a definite "no," but remain willing to consider various possibilities.
6. *Present conclusions as if they are joint agreements.* Look for opportunities to make comments such as, "As you say . . ." and "As you suggested . . ."
7. *Don't argue back and forth.* Arguing is counterproductive to the win/win process.

DISCUSSION SCENARIO: MRS. LANGLOIS NEEDS SUPPLIES FOR HER CLASSROOM

Mrs. Langlois, a second-year teacher, has just been transferred from one school to another because of unanticipated changes in enrollment. She has left the class she thought she'd have, a second grade, and is assigned to teach fourth grade. She arrives with only two days to prepare her classroom and curriculum. When shown her classroom she is dismayed to find that while it contains textbooks, maps, and a globe, there are no instructional materials such as paper, scissors, paste, construction paper, butcher paper, pencils, markers, art supplies, science materials, reference books, or other reading materials suitable for her students. She makes an appointment to see the school principal, Mr. Markz. Mr. Markz has already anticipated her visit. He has found $100 in discretionary funds he can make available to her. He knows the amount won't begin to cover her needs, but feels she can make up shortages through her own initiative. Any additional money she needs must come out of her own pocket.

Mrs. Langlois has learned from other teachers that Mr. Markz is a principal strong on school discipline and keeping costs down, but is not overly sympathetic to teachers' needs. He is said to be very outspoken and opinionated. She is told that he thinks teachers did just fine when they had only textbooks, chalk, and a blackboard and sees no reason why they feel they need many materials that are costly and ineffective.

Suppose you are Mrs. Langlois. How do you approach Mr. Markz? Do you ask him to consider the suggestions made for a win/win resolution? How do you express your needs so you might persuade him to provide additional help?

Suppose you are Mr. Markz. You are anticipating Mrs. Langlois's visit and request. How do you speak with her so she will understand your position?

Suppose you are a neutral person mediating the conflict between Mrs. Langlois and Mr. Markz. Can you see any possibility of a win/win resolution to this conflict?

A FINAL OBSERVATION

Stephen R. Covey (1989, p. 207) writes:

> Win/win is a frame of mind and heart that constantly seeks mutual benefit in all human interactions. Win/win means that agreements or solutions are mutually beneficial, mutually satisfying. With a win/win solution, all parties feel good about the decision and feel committed to the action plan. Win/win sees life as a cooperative, not a competitive arena.
>
> Win/win is based on the paradigm that there is plenty for everybody, that one person's success is not achieved at the expense or exclusion of the success of others.
>
> Win/win is a belief in the Third Alternative. It's not your way or my way; it's a *better* way, a higher way.

Win/win solutions to conflict are one of the major accomplishments we strive for in synergetic teaching and discipline. If we can achieve their positive results, teaching becomes more joyous while classroom problems fade to little more than temporary inconveniences.

WHERE DO WE GO FROM HERE?

In this chapter we have seen how nondisciplinary problems and conflicts are resolved in a manner that preserves personal dignity, motivation, and personal relations. We saw that problems are different from conflicts in that the latter involve clashes of will and strong emotion. Problems are solved by the entire class pulling together to remove an obstacle or achieve a goal. Conflicts are resolved by seeking out common-ground possibilities that allow both sides in the dispute to feel they have achieved most of what they wanted.

This completes our consideration of the nine elements that combine to produce class synergy. In the next chapter we explore how discipline problems and conflicts are resolved humanely and nonpunitively in the synergetic classroom.

To Think About

1. What distinction do you now make between a "problem" and a "conflict?" Given the distinction, do you see why they are resolved differently?
2. Think of problem situations you are now contending with or have contended with recently in your personal life. What information have you obtained from the chapter that might help you deal with similar situations more effectively?
3. Think of a conflict situation you have experienced in the recent past. Was the conflict resolved in a manner satisfactory to you? To the other person(s) involved? Were good relationships maintained? If the resolution or relationships were not satisfactory, what might you have done differently?
4. Suppose you find yourself in a troublesome conflict. You understand the process of win/win resolution but the other person does not. What, if anything, might you do to enlighten the other person so the two of you can approach the discussion in the same manner?

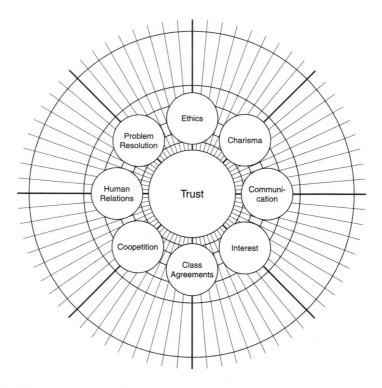

Figure 9.8   The synergy sunburst.

Gentle Discipline in the Synergetic Classroom

Mr. Phelps always encouraged students to solve
class problems on their own.

The Fiery Miss Coldwell

Miss Coldwell, my trigonometry teacher, was the archetypical old-style disciplinarian. She could be (and often was) the personification of wrath, backing her fierceness with allusions to unspeakable consequences for those who defied her. I dreamed one night I saw fire shooting from her nose and there was no doubt in my mind her voice could shatter windows and walls. That was many years ago, you understand. I came to know Miss Coldwell socially a few years afterward and found her rather charming. It was as if there had been a mix-up. The genteel Miss Coldwell of later years could hardly have been the outrageous harpy that struck fear into so many adolescent hearts.

Miss Coldwell's style of discipline, though memorable, was hardly unique among teachers of her day. Up into the 1970s most teachers used searing voice and dire threat to keep students in line. Some try it still, but with little effect because students now shrug it off. As you know, students are not much afraid of teachers anymore, which is a good thing. They also know (more's the pity) that instead of receiving additional grief at home for what they do wrong at school, their parents will usually side with them against school and teacher. So what do we do now when a student defies us? Send him to the principal's office? The student's reaction will probably be: Hey, thanks, good change of scenery. Do we schedule her to see the counselor? The reaction will probably be: Right. I'm looking forward to the chat.

TODAY'S MISBEHAVIOR: HOW SERIOUS IS IT?

In order to have a complete perspective from which to explore discipline in the synergetic classroom, we need to appraise current conditions regarding student behavior and review modern efforts to deal with it. We begin by considering today's misbehavior.

Day in and day out, student misbehavior is the most troublesome problem teachers face. Most teachers have to deal with it all day long every day. For a few who are lucky or skilled, misbehavior may be only a minor annoyance. (Those teachers usually enjoy their jobs very much.) For teachers less fortunate, misbehavior can become sufficiently demoralizing to destroy their professional lives—inability to keep misbehavior within reasonable bounds is the principal cause of teacher failure, and continually having to deal with misbehavior burns out teachers and drives them away from the profession.

WHAT CONSTITUTES MISBEHAVIOR?

Misbehavior does not have a precise definition, but there is fairly close agreement about its meaning. We have said that misbehavior is intentional behavior that runs contrary to class agreements. Note the qualifier "intentional": The perpetrator knows the act is not approved but does it anyway. There are four types of such behavior:

1. *Benign disruption*. Behaviors in this category include talking or laughing inappropriately and moving about the classroom without permission. These behaviors don't often involve hostility, aggression, or defiance and thus are not threatening. They are annoying, however, and disruptive enough to interfere with teaching and learning. Most teachers have to contend with this kind of misbehavior continually.

2. *Withdrawal from learning*. Behaviors in this category include daydreaming instead of working, failure to participate in class activities, and unwillingness to do assigned work. Teachers are not overly troubled when one or two students behave in this manner, but when one-third or more disengage they have real reason for concern. William Glasser concluded as early as 1986 that "no more than half of our secondary school students are willing to make an effort to learn, and therefore cannot be taught." (1986, p. 3) In 1990 he wrote that the secondary teachers he spoke with said they yearned to work with dedicated high-achieving students but were continually frustrated by the

majority who made little effort. The apathy Glasser wrote about several years ago has not improved. It continues to frustrate secondary teachers. Elementary teachers now complain about it too.

3. *Immorality and indecency.* Behaviors in this category are acts that are disapproved because they violate societal mores. They include cheating, lying, stealing, intimidating others, sexual innuendo, and sexual harassment. Some of these behaviors, such as lying and stealing, are evident in young students when they enter school. Cheating and intimidation become noticeable in the middle elementary grades, while sexual innuendo and harassment are usually first reported in late elementary grades. All continue through secondary school. They are difficult to deal with but only occasionally interfere with teaching.

4. *Hostile confrontations.* Behaviors in this category include verbal and physical aggression, bullying, fighting, and overt resistance to teacher requests. These are the behaviors that trouble teachers most. Students may fight. They may hostilely resist teachers and may swear at them. Occasionally they attack teachers physically. Fortunately, these dire behaviors occur infrequently. The worst most teachers will ever see is squabbling and an occasional scuffle.

WHY DO STUDENTS MISBEHAVE?

Students misbehave for many different reasons. These reasons may be thought of as causes of misbehavior. Identifying the cause is important because if we can correct it, we can control the misbehavior. Causes of misbehavior include:

1. *Probing boundaries.* It is challenging for some students to probe the boundaries of acceptable behavior, especially when they have not been closely involved in establishing them. When they probe, they sometimes transgress. Their behaviors are seldom malicious but are frequently disruptive.

2. *Mimicking others.* Younger students are highly imitative and often try to outdo each other. A behavior that is not disruptive in itself may be imitated and in the process grow to unacceptable proportions.

3. *Strong curiosity or interest.* Students may be so curious about or deeply interested in something that they disregard agreements that stand in the way of satisfying the curiosity or interest.

4. *Desire for attention.* Some students clamor for attention. They may seek it from the teacher or other students. When they cannot get it through legitimate means, they get it by misbehaving.

5. *Desire for power.* Practically all students want some power in school. Most are satisfied when allowed to help make decisions that affect the class. Others, particularly those who have not been able to get adequate attention, try to show power by defying the teacher. When the teacher asks something of them, they drag their feet, complain, or refuse to comply.

6. *Boredom or frustration.* Students quickly disengage from tasks they find boring, meaningless, or frustrating. They then look for something more interesting to do, such as daydreaming or talking and joking with others.

7. *Overly emotional from something that happened outside of class.* Students may at times become so emotional they lose their willingness to abide by class agreements. They may withdraw from activities and speak inappropriately to others.

8. *Threat to dignity.* When students' sense of self is threatened they typically do one of three things—they withdraw behind defenses that shut others out, lie or cheat to cover inadequacies or deflect blame, or react with verbal or physical aggression. All of these are serious behaviors and all work against class synergy.

9. *Disagreements that boil over.* Students sometimes have minor disagreements that under normal circumstances are forgotten or resolved amicably. Sometimes, however, those disagreements fester until they boil over into aggression.

10. *Egocentric personality.* We regularly come in contact with students who have overblown egos. They feel whatever they do is right. Some have been spoiled and act out when they don't get their way. Some feel there is nothing much wrong with lying, cheating, and stealing. Misbehavior caused by personality traits is difficult to deal with. Teachers can best exert positive influence over these students by constantly displaying ethical behavior, working to build trust, and discussing the inappropriateness of egocentric behavior.

We should note that causes 3, 4, 5, 6, and 8 can stem from an incompatibility between instruction and student nature. In Chapter 6 we identified several predominant student traits and saw how instruction often runs contrary to them. When this incompatibility exists, students do not engage willingly in the activities teachers provide. Teachers then try to force student compliance. Force does not work. Even when it seems effective it produces apathy, withdrawal, frustration, dissatisfaction, resistance, dislike for the teacher, and dislike for school, all of which are emotional seedbeds for misbehavior. This need not happen. It is not difficult to organize instruction to meet student needs, as shown later in Figure 10.1.

THE SYNERGETIC CLASSROOM REMOVES MOST CAUSES OF MISBEHAVIOR

In most classes, insufficient effort is given to minimizing the known causes of misbehavior. Students are not given the attention and power they seek. Instruction is not nearly as interesting as it could be. Teachers unknowingly damage student dignity and provoke reactions by using harsh tones, threats, and sarcasm. Only an occasional teacher organizes instruction so it satisfies student needs for the following:

- Security—safety from threat and abuse in a place of one's own
- Hope—belief that school will be helpful and that success is possible
- Acceptance—sense of belonging gained through acknowledgment and recognition
- Dignity—respectful sense of self, whole and intact
- Power—control over some of the educational decisions in the class
- Enjoyment—pleasure from the process and results of learning
- Competence—becoming very knowledgeable or skillful

When striving for synergy, teachers give every student attention and acceptance. They make instructional activities highly appealing so students will participate willingly and enjoy their experience. They relate to students in ways that build trust and dignity. They stress good personal relations and teach students how to resolve problems and conflicts. As they do these things, they remove most of the conditions that lead to misbehavior. These teachers do not think of discipline as something they do to students to make them behave, but something they do in teaching to help students accept instruction and profit from it. Students treated in this way acquire a pattern of positive behavior that serves them all their lives.

HOW WE HAVE ARRIVED AT THIS POINT IN DISCIPLINE

The synergetic approach makes teaching joyful and discipline easy. Unfortunately, it cannot eliminate all discipline problems. Despite our best efforts we always encounter a few students who do not respond to kind, helpful treatment. And we teachers are human, too—we can't always be impeccably positive and do or say the proper things. When misbehavior occurs we have to deal with it. When we do, we want to accomplish two ends—redirect the misbehavior appropriately and maintain positive relations with the student. Later in this chapter you will find suggestions for doing this. But first let's take a moment to review how classroom discipline has evolved over the past half-century. The following chronology highlights pivotal points. As you read, note how suggested methods of dealing with misbehavior have progressively changed.

The Old-Fashioned Approach

From the beginnings of teaching right up to recent years, educators used a fairly standard way of dealing with misbehavior, not unlike that of my former teacher Miss Coldwell. They tried to make students afraid to misbehave and punished them when they did. Their tactics included cold demeanor, cutting tone of voice, threat, psychological domination, and various kinds of punishment. There were exceptions of course, but that's how most teachers kept students under control. That approach was fairly effective so long as students cared what happened to them and teachers had the backing of parents. But student caring and parental backing began to crumble in the 1960s. Since then, old-fashioned discipline has become less and less effective. Now it does more harm than good.

The Beginning of Modern Discipline

In 1951, Fritz Redl and William Wattenberg published *Mental Hygiene in Teaching*, in which they set forth the first organized "new approach" to discipline. They advised teachers to quickly assess misbehavior and clarify four things—what caused the behavior, how the class is reacting, how the student will react when corrected, and how the correction will affect the student's future behavior. Teachers should then apply the most appropriate of the following procedures: (1) Support the student's self-control—through sending signals and moving close to the student; (2) Provide situational assistance—help the student deal with the condition that provoked the misbehavior; (3) Appraise reality—give students encouragement and remind them of the penalties for misbehavior; or (4) Invoke the pleasure–pain principle—meaning punish the offender.

Behavior Modification

Beginning in the 1930s and continuing for more than three decades, behavioral psychologist B. F. Skinner investigated how animal and human behavior could be modified through the application of reinforcing stimuli. The process involved waiting for the organism to behave in a desired manner and then immediately giving it a reinforcer, usually a bit of food. Skinner found that this process could be used to teach new, complex behavior in both laboratory animals and humans. In the middle 1960s, educators used Skinner's findings to devise a procedure for shaping student behavior. They called it behavior modification. Instead of food as the reinforcing stimulus, they used praise, marks, and tangible objects such as stars and toys. When teachers saw students behaving as desired, they thanked or praised them. This caused students to behave in a yet more desirable manner. Behavior modification is still used today, though usually as one of several elements in a more encompassing discipline system. It is most successful with young children and the intellectually disadvantaged.

Democratic Teaching

Rudolf Dreikurs (1972, with Pearl Cassel) published *Discipline Without Tears*, in which he pushed strongly for developing self-discipline in students which he believed could be accomplished through "democratic teaching," emphasizing respectfulness toward students and involving them in making decisions about class matters. He said true discipline is self-generated respectfulness based on social interest— that is, students learn that proper behavior contributes to the quality of personal and social life (Dreikurs, Grunwald & Pepper, 1998). Every student has a need to belong and that discipline problems occur when the student is unable to meet that need. He believed most discipline problems disappear when students feel they belong in class and school and are allowed to give input into decisions that affect them.

Congruent Communication

In 1971 Haim Ginott published *Teacher and Child*, a very influential book in education. As described in Chapter 4, he set forth the concept of congruent communication—communication that is harmonious with students' feelings about situations and themselves. Teachers who use congruent communication in discipline address situations but not the character of the student. They do not blame, command, preach, belittle, or threaten. They only comment calmly on what needs to be done. Ginott described discipline as a series of little victories by which teachers gain the goodwill of students. Those victories are won by conferring dignity, accepting and acknowledging feelings, never labeling or otherwise attacking students, and always being polite, helpful, and respectful. Ginott wanted teachers continually to ask themselves, "What can I do right now that will be of most benefit to my students?"

Assertive Discipline

In 1976 Lee Canter and Marlene Canter published their blockbuster *Assertive Discipline: A Take-Charge Approach for Today's Educator.* This book took the discipline world by storm. The Canters told teachers they have a right to teach, and students have a right to learn, without disruptions from misbehavior. They provided a detailed strategy to apply when students misbehave. First, rules for class behavior are established. When students break a rule, the teacher applies a preestablished hierarchy of consequences, beginning with a warning. If the student fails to comply, the teacher invokes progressively more severe consequences until the misbehavior ceases. The teacher does this in a calm, matter-of-fact manner, without becoming upset. Despite its popularity Assertive Discipline was earlier criticized as too stern, too focused on forcing students to comply, too harsh especially for young children, and ineffective in encouraging self-discipline. Lee and Marlene Canter addressed those criticisms by adding components on building trust and respect, teaching students how they were expected to behave, and redirecting nondisruptive misbehavior. They also added techniques for working with difficult-to-manage students (Canter & Canter, 1993).

Discipline as Self-Control

Thomas Gordon first gained fame as the author of *Parent Effectiveness Training* (1970) and *T.E.T.: Teacher Effectiveness Training* (1974). In 1989 he published *Discipline That Works: Promoting Self-Discipline in Children.* He says the goal of discipline is to establish self-control in learners. He calls on teachers to abandon punishment, praise, rewards, and behavior modification. He contends that punishment of any sort reduces motivation and desire to cooperate while increasing lying and cheating. He says praise and rewards are ineffective: Students work just for the reward and feel punished if it is not forthcoming. If the reward is removed they return to undesirable behavior. Gordon urges teachers to replace threat and coercion with preventive skills, helping skills, and confrontive skills. Preventive skills include class agreements and participative decision making. Helping skills include passive and active listening, acknowledgment, and avoidance of comments that interfere with communication. Confrontive skills include identifying and modifying the cause of misbehavior, sending I-messages, and using methods of win/win conflict resolution.

Noncoercive Discipline

Few writers of the late twentieth century have influenced education more than William Glasser, who rose to prominence with his 1965 book *Reality Therapy: A New Approach to Psychiatry.* In 1969 Glasser published *Schools Without Failure*, which introduced three concepts new to teaching: (1) Most students choose to behave as they do; nothing forces them, (2) A sense of failure is extremely detrimental to students, and (3) Problems that affect teacher and students should be worked out collaboratively in class meetings. In 1986 he published *Control Theory in the Classroom.* He had found that students were becoming progressively less interested in school and none of the discipline methods in vogue could force their interest. He therefore turned to teaching as the most viable avenue for improving behavior. He said the curriculum and teaching could not be successful unless they met students' needs for belonging, power, fun, and freedom. When those needs are not met, students misbehave or disengage from the educational process. When the needs *are* met in the classroom, students engage in learning and have little reason to misbehave.

Beyond Discipline

Alfie Kohn published in 1996 a provocative book entitled *Beyond Discipline: From Compliance to Community.* In that book, he contends that teachers should forget about discipline as such and focus instead on building a sense of community in the class. He particularly dislikes rewarding and punishing students, which he says teaches them to distrust their own perception. Furthermore, rewards and praise do not cause students to feel any commitment to learning, but only interest in receiving the reward. Classroom communities are places where everybody is cared for and cares about each other, where everyone thinks in terms of *we* rather than *I*. When problems arise, the teacher asks the class, "What do you think we can do to resolve this problem?" In rare instances when control over students must be exerted (e.g., for their safety or because they are being cruel to each other), teachers should make sure students understand the reason control is being used.

OTHER KEY CONTRIBUTORS

The people whose views were described in the previous paragraphs have been pivotal in development of discipline. All of them introduced significant new ideas of lasting influence (Alfie Kohn's ideas have yet to meet the test of time). In addition to those authorities, several others are playing strong roles today in helping improve school discipline. With the exception of Jacob Kounin, all of the following people are actively promoting their programs through books, videos, journal articles, conference addresses, and workshops. While their ideas may not have broken new ground to the extent of those featured previously, their efforts to improve conditions for teachers and students deserve mention.

Kounin's Lesson Management

Jacob Kounin, in his book *Discipline and Group Management in Classrooms* (1971), presented his research on how the management of class routines and the presentation of lessons affect student behavior. He concluded that keeping students actively involved in learning with no wasted time is the best way to maintain good discipline.

Jones's Positive Classroom Discipline

Fredric Jones, in his 1987 book *Positive Classroom Discipline*, champions the use of body language. He says teachers' most effective discipline tool is their body language (such as eye contact, physical proximity, gestures, and facial expressions). He also claims that incentive systems (such as all students behaving well in order to earn a class treat) can help the class take responsibility for proper behavior.

Albert's Cooperative Discipline

Linda Albert in her 1996 book *Cooperative Discipline* explains how to reduce discipline problems by helping all students feel they belong. She advocates showing students they are capable, interconnected with each other, and able to contribute meaningfully to the class. She suggests using a class code of conduct formulated in collaboration with students and parents.

Nelsen, Lott, and Glenn's Positive Discipline

Jane Nelsen, Lynn Lott, and H. Stephen Glenn, in their book *Positive Discipline in the Classroom* (1997), describe an approach that puts faith in students' ability to control themselves, cooperate, assume responsibility, and behave in a dignified manner. Students learn how to collaborate in solving problems, are provided a learning environment that instills excitement for learning, and are never subjected to humiliation.

Curwin and Mendler's Discipline with Dignity
Richard Curwin and Allen Mendler have described strategies teachers can use to enhance student dignity and instill hope. Their book *Discipline With Dignity* (1988) highlights student dignity and explains why it should always be taken into account. Curwin, in his book *Rediscovering Hope: Our Greatest Teaching Strategy* (1992), provides strategies for working effectively with at-risk students—those whose behavior would normally cause them to fail in school.

Coloroso's Inner Discipline
Barbara Coloroso, in *Kids Are Worth It!: Giving Your Child The Gift of Inner Discipline* (1994), presents suggestions for helping students develop inner discipline, which she defines as the ability to behave creatively, constructively, cooperatively, and responsibly without being directed by an adult. When teachers discipline students, they should show students what they have done wrong, give them ownership of the problem they have created, help them resolve the problem, and allow their dignity to remain intact.

WHAT WE HAVE LEARNED FROM THESE AUTHORITIES AND THEIR CONTRIBUTIONS

Old-fashioned discipline doesn't work anymore. Teachers who lay down the law unilaterally and try to make students comply are doomed to frustration and disillusionment. Their students will resist learning, dislike school, and either misbehave or withdraw.

Student self-discipline is what we are seeking. With self-discipline, students behave acceptably because they feel it proper and to their advantage to do so. Teachers, by giving up power techniques in favor of influence techniques, remove themselves from a controlling role in favor of helping students develop self-discipline.

Misbehavior declines when students look upon the class as a family. When students think of classmates as brothers and sisters, each becomes concerned about the welfare of the others. Though they won't always see eye to eye, they take care of each other. The more capable help the less capable. Those with problems have supportive classmates to lean on. The class as a whole does not allow anyone to be slighted or feel diminished.

In discipline, gentle approaches are more effective than harsh approaches. Gentle, positive, persuasive approaches encourage proper behavior far better than do stern voice, threat, and punishment. Today's students rebel against harsh treatment, but can be won over through kindness and respect.

It is essential that we meet students' needs. Students will behave properly and try to learn when we make school satisfy their needs for

Put These Factors in Place	Aim Activities At	Provide One or More of These
Security	Enjoyment	Novelty
Hope	Competence	Mystery
Dignity		Drama
Acceptance		Challenge
Power		Coopetition

Figure 10.1 Organizing school and instruction to meet student needs.

security, acceptance, hope, dignity, power, enjoyment, and competence. Figure 10.1 shows how to organize to meet student needs.

Good relationships between teacher and students reduce discipline problems and make those that occur easier to deal with. We win trust through the way we treat students. Examine the teacher demeanors shown in Figure 10.2. Each time the teacher shows demeanor in the positive category, trust is built up with the student. Each time the teacher shows demeanor in the negative category, trust is lost.

When students are interested and involved in lessons, they seldom misbehave. Behavior problems are greatly reduced when teachers keep students involved by providing interesting lessons on meaningful topics. Refer back to Figure 10.1.

Students' dignity is affected by how the teacher speaks to them. Building and maintaining student dignity should be given top priority. Teachers confer dignity by being attentive and respectful and by using congruent communication, which addresses situations rather than the character of the student.

Students should collaborate in making decisions about the class. Students are more likely to comply with standards of conduct and other expectations when, first, they collaborate meaningfully in making the decisions and, second, when they see that compliance with decisions benefits the group and themselves.

When students misbehave, we should identify and correct whatever is causing the misbehavior. Figure 10.3 lists causes of misbehavior and the

Positive: Build Trust	Negative: Erode Trust
Friendly	Distant
Kind	Cold
Acknowledges	Slights
Invites	Coerces
Makes suggestions	Gives orders
Encourages	Demands
Helpful	Disinterested
Listens	Disregards
Appreciates	Criticizes
Considerate	Indifferent
Respects	Demeans

Figure 10.2 Teacher demeanors that build and erode trust.

Causes of Misbehavior	Dealing with the Causes
• Probing limits	• Class agreements, reminder
• Mimicking others	• Class agreements, reminder
• Strong curiosity or interest	• Class agreements, reminder with consideration
• Desire for attention	• Consistently provide attention to all students
• Desire for power	• Allow students to collaborate in class decisions
• Boredom or frustration	• Make all lessons interesting and doable
• Emotionality	• Calmly chat with the student; show consideration
• Threat to dignity	• Class agreements; chat with the student
• Disagreements that boil over	• Conflict resolution
• Egocentric personality	• Ethical example, trust, and discussion

Figure 10.3   Causes of misbehavior and how to deal with them.

best ways to approach the causes in order to correct them. The causes can often be eliminated by the teacher or at least modified through problem and conflict resolution.

THE APPROACH TO SYNERGETIC DISCIPLINE

We move now to a consideration of synergetic discipline and how it is accomplished in the classroom. Discipline in the synergetic classroom is used only to help students. It is never used to denigrate, scold, or punish. We know that anything we do that damages student dignity will come back to haunt us; it will cause the student to harbor resentment toward us, become less willing to cooperate, and dislike the class and school. When misbehavior occurs we intervene positively. We take care to support the student, show respect, and provide help. This does not mean we tolerate misbehavior that is damaging to the student, to other students, or to us. To the contrary, we do not permit it. In the synergetic classroom, we do everything possible to minimize misbehavior. But when it does occur, we *deal with its cause* in a helpful, dignified manner. When we are able to identify the cause, we can usually remove or correct it. When we do that, the misbehavior ceases.

How do we do this? Though discipline in the synergetic classroom is extraordinarily effective, the process is not cut-and-dry. It uses no pre-established intervention strategy. There is no set of steps to follow when discipline problems occur. What you decide to do is a matter of personal choice, based on what you consider best for particular students at a particular time, tempered by your personality. If you are uncertain how to begin, you might find the following suggestions helpful.

Ongoing Tasks

There are three tasks you need to accomplish as quickly as possible, beginning the first day of class. As you accomplish these tasks you establish conditions that foster synergetic discipline. The *first task* is to formulate a set of **class agreements** about behavior, teaching, and learning. Establishing a set of agreements requires considerable thought and discussion by the class, whose full input is essential. The agreements when finalized may be stated succinctly, including perhaps no more than the following (worded appropriately for the age of your students):

In our class, teacher and students all agree to:

1. Make learning enjoyable and satisfying.
2. Treat others with courtesy and respect at all times.
3. Try to do our best work always.
4. Solve our problems with others in a polite, respectful manner.

These agreements are further clarified through example and role-playing.

The *second task* is to begin developing a **sense of family** in the class, where students help and look out for each other. This sense of family can be initiated in the first days of the class and will become well established over time, but you need to remind the class frequently of its importance.

The *third task* is to begin conscientiously **putting into practice** the nine elements of synergetic teaching—ethics, trust, charisma, communication, interest, class agreements, coopetition, human relations, and problem resolution. It will take several weeks to bring all nine elements to full functioning.

As these three tasks are completed and kept in place, most discipline concerns you would otherwise experience do not appear.

Dealing with Misbehavior

It would be wonderful if your ongoing efforts eliminated misbehavior altogether. Unfortunately the synergetic approach doesn't quite accomplish that goal, though it certainly reduces misbehavior greatly. You will at times have to deal with students whose behavior transgresses the class agreements. For decades teachers have found that duty unpleasant, tiring, and wasteful of time. The synergetic approach not only reduces the frequency of misbehavior but also removes most of the attendant tension and trauma. You might find these suggestions helpful:

1. *When misbehavior is perceived, look immediately for its cause.* Misbehavior is what we call student acts that intentionally violate class agreements. It always has a cause. The cause may be apparent (e.g., students have begun to fidget and daydream because they find the lesson boring) or it may be hidden (e.g. Nathan and Jason speak angrily to each other, causing students to stop work—you do not know what has provoked the exchange). Even if you think you know the cause, check with students before proceeding. Mistaking the cause of misbehavior can lead to errors in dealing with students. You might ask, "Are you feeling bored?" If the cause is not apparent, try to get information from those involved. Don't scold Nathan and Jason but gently ask, "Boys, is there a problem I can help with?"

Remind the students that it is very difficult to make fair decisions without all the facts.

2. *When the problem is identified, correct the cause if possible.* The cause can almost always be eliminated or modified. If the lesson is so boring it is causing students to disengage, either end it, change something about it, or ask students to stick with it for a bit longer. Here are things you might say:

- (To end the boredom) I think you've had about all this activity you can take. Let's stop here. Perhaps you can help me clarify what there is about the lesson that makes it unappealing.
- (To modify the boredom) I can tell you are getting tired, but I think it's important to complete the assignment. Would you like to work with a partner? Maybe you can put your minds together and complete the work more easily.
- (To request perseverance) Class, we are almost done. I know you are tired, but if you can stay with me for two more minutes we'll have the lesson completed. I'd very much appreciate your cooperation.

3. *If the misbehavior leads to a confrontation, correct the cause by seeking a solution.* The confrontation might be between students or between a student and yourself. Here are some ways you might consider dealing with the conflict.

    Between Students. Suppose during a lesson you see Jason and Nathan speaking angrily to each other. You might wish to say:

- Can you boys work this out between yourselves or do you need my help? (If they say they can work it out themselves, ask them to keep their dispute from affecting others in the class. Also ask them if they might feel like telling you later what they have decided.)
- If the conflict is such that they can't resolve it, you might do the following:

(1) Ask each to tell you calmly what is troubling them. (By this means you learn that Nathan has twice taken a pen from Jason's desk and has refused to return it. Nathan claims Jason owes him money and is refusing to repay it, so Nathan feels entitled to the pens.)

(2) Ask Jason what he would like Nathan to do differently. Nathan listens carefully.

(3) Ask Nathan what he would like Jason to do differently. Jason listens carefully.

(4) Ask the boys if each feels he could do part or all of what the other says he would like.

(5) Reach an agreement, if possible. Ask each of the boys if they feel they can abide by their agreement and feel all right about it. Ask

them if they can now put the dispute behind them. If they say yes, thank them sincerely.

(6) If they are unable to reach an agreement, ask if they would mind if the class discussed their incident in a class meeting in order to learn more about maintaining good relations in the class.

(7) If they give permission, bring the matter up for discussion at the next class meeting. If they do not give permission, say:

- Jason and Nathan, we need to settle this. It is not good for any of us in the class when bad feelings exist. How can we resolve this matter satisfactorily for both of you? What ideas do you have?

(8) If the boys cannot find a way to resolve the conflict, consider saying:

- I'm disappointed we can't settle this matter so you both feel satisfied. But since we can't, I need to ask you to control yourselves. Try to put your differences aside. For the sake of our class don't allow your feelings to boil over so they affect the rest of us. (Note: It is extremely unlikely that the conflict between Jason and Nathan would ever reach this point. They would resolve it earlier in the process.)

Between Student and Teacher. *(Melissa has failed to do her homework once again. You ask her kindly if there is a problem that is preventing her from doing the assigned work. Your comment for some reason strikes a nerve and Melissa retorts, "There wouldn't be a problem if you didn't assign the stupid stuff!")* When a student speaks to you in this manner you might consider replying as follows:

- Melissa, can you help me understand why you think the homework is stupid? I'd like your opinion because I thought the work would be helpful in improving your understanding. What can you tell me about it? Melissa may apologize, say nothing, come back with another snide remark, or give you an explanation for her feelings. If she says nothing or remains hostile, you might wish to say:
- Now is not a good time for us to discuss the matter. Perhaps we can do so later, just the two of us. Could you meet with me for a minute or two at (name a time and place)? At the meeting you might want to mention your suspicion that something other than the homework is troubling her, but you are unable to guess what it might be. Tell her you are willing to listen if she has something she needs to talk about. If she declines, assure her you are interested in her appraisal of the homework and ready to help if she is experiencing problems with it.

If she apologizes or explains her feelings, consider saying:

- Thank you, Melissa. If I can make good changes in the homework or help with your situation, I'd like to do so. Do you have suggestions?

SUMMARY OF SUGGESTIONS FOR DISCIPLINE IN THE SYNERGETIC CLASSROOM

Figure 10.4 summarizes suggestions concerning discipline in the synergetic classroom.

DISCIPLINE SCENARIOS FOR YOUR CONSIDERATION

Here are some additional behavior situations for you to consider. They are given in pairs—part *a* and part *b*. Part *a* in each pair shows how the teacher deals with the problem. Part *b* in each pair asks how you would deal with it if in the teacher's shoes.

Scenario #1a. Hernán

The class has just viewed a video showing how a school worked to clean the debris from a small stream that ran through the community. Mr. Akers has asked the class members to identify a project along those lines that might be good for the class to undertake. He has asked each student to think of possibilities and make notes for sharing ideas with the class. He notices after 10 minutes that Hernán is gazing out the window. He walks by Hernán's desk and sees that no notes have been made. Is this a problem? Is it a discipline problem? What should Mr. Akers say to Hernán, if anything?

Mr. Akers determined he needed to help Hernán. He considered it a discipline problem because the class had agreed they would always do their best work and Hernán was not working at all. He quietly asked Hernán if he was having trouble. Hernán replied honestly that his mind was on something else. Mr. Akers asked, "Can you for the next 10 minutes give full attention to the assignment? There is still time to finish if you hurry." Hernán began to write notes on his paper.

The philosophy of synergetic discipline: Always be helpful, never hurtful.

Ongoing efforts: These are initiated early and kept in a place thereafter.
   1. Establish a set of class agreements.
   2. Develop a sense of family, where everyone looks out for everyone else.
   3. Put into practice the nine elements needed for class synergy.

Dealing with misbehavior:
   1. Look for the cause. Don't jump to conclusions. Try to get the facts straight.
   2. Correct the cause, if possible, by eliminating or modifying it.
   3. Deal positively with confrontations.
      Between students: Try for win/win resolution.
      Between student and teacher: Hear the student out and make modifications to relieve the concern, if possible.

Figure 10.4 Suggestions concerning discipline in the synergetic classroom.

Scenario #1b. Ella

Mrs. Nguyen's students had been studying about Vietnam. As a culminating assignment, she asked students to write a theme on the lives of the farmers of the Mekong Delta. When the assignments were turned in the following week, Mrs. Nguyen saw that Ella's paper was beautifully rendered using word-processing software. That pleased her, but when she began to read she realized Ella's paper contained words and concepts too advanced for her level. She immediately suspected that Ella had copied the material from a reference book on Southeast Asia that was in the school library. She located the book and found the material in Ella's paper almost identical to that in the book.

Is this a problem? Is it a discipline problem? If you were Mrs. Nguyen, how would you approach Ella with your concern? How would you attempt to resolve the problem so Ella meets your standards yet retains her dignity? (This question is broached again in "To Think About" at the end of this chapter.)

Scenario #2a. Shawon

Shawon is new to Miss Gillette's first-grade class. The class has learned to raise their hands before speaking. Shawon, however, blurts out answers to all Miss Gillette's questions without raising his hand. At the beginning of the lesson, Miss Gillette had reviewed the class agreement about raising hands before speaking. Now she repeats it to Shawon. Only a minute passes before Shawon again shouts out an answer.

This is a problem because it violates class agreements and bothers Miss Gillette and others in the class. It will be a discipline problem if it continues for another day or two, but for now Miss Gillette does not believe Shawon is intentionally violating the agreement. She believes he gets excited and forgets. At a class meeting later in the day she reviews the agreement and has the class role-play situations where they should raise their hands. She notes that Shawon raises his hand appropriately.

Scenario #2b. Clarisse

While Mrs. Cousins is instructing a reading group, Clarisse who is supposed to be doing seatwork gets up from her desk and wanders back to the aquarium. Mrs. Cousins quietly calls her name, smiles, and nods toward Clarisse's desk. She goes back. A few minutes later Mrs. Cousins notices that Clarisse has returned to the aquarium.

Is this a problem? Is it a discipline problem? If you were Mrs. Cousins, how would you approach Clarisse with your concern?

Scenario #3a. Valerio and Mack

In gym class the students have dressed out and are making their way onto the court for volleyball. Mr. Grey comes from the locker room just in time to see Valerio and Mack square off. Valerio pushes Mack and Mack staggers to the floor. He jumps up and goes half-heartedly after

Valerio. Mr. Grey separates the boys. He sees that Valerio is smouldering. Mack looks sheepish.

This is a discipline problem for Mr. Grey as it violates agreements about no fighting or scuffling. He asks the other students to begin playing in their assigned teams and takes Valerio and Mack to the side where he can talk while overseeing the others. He says to the boys, "Fellows, fighting is serious and violates our agreements. We need to get this matter resolved calmly and respectfully. I'll help you if I can but first I need to know what the problem is. Valerio, what can you tell me about it?"

Valerio says Mack had been taunting him about being fat while they were getting dressed and wouldn't stop and it carried on into the gym. Mack adds that the two of them had been joking about other matters and let their comments become too personal. Mr. Grey says, "I appreciate your telling me. Now how can we take care of it? I'd like to hear your ideas. Mack, you speak first this time. What do you see as the problem and how can we solve it?"

Mack says he is mostly to blame and is sorry because Valerio is a friend. He says he'll not call Valerio names anymore. Mr. Grey says, "Valerio, what do you have to say?" Valerio says things just got out of hand and he knows fighting is not acceptable and he won't do it again.

Mr. Grey asks, "Have both of you calmed down? Can you put this incident behind you and remain friends?" The boys say they can. They trot over to join their teams.

Scenario #3b. Shane

While on playground duty during sixth-grade recess, Miss Banfill hears abusive talk from Shane, a big robust boy, directed at Mark who is small and nonassertive. She hears Shane call Mark a shrimp and yell at him to stay out of the way. The verbal abuse from Shane continues and Miss Banfill decides to intervene. Suppose you are Miss Banfill. Describe how you would deal with the situation if (a) Shane seems contrite, and (b) If Shane speaks back to you argumentatively.

Scenario #4a. Heather and Christine

Heather and Christine are members of the school yearbook committee. Each member is in charge of a particular aspect of the yearbook but all give input during planning. In the early stages the committee has free-flowing discussions concerning a possible theme and how they wish to organize the book. Ms. Philippoussis is the yearbook sponsor who guides the group's work. In the first meeting, committee members use profanity occasionally. Ms. Philippoussis doesn't comment about it. By the third meeting, the level of profanity has increased. Suddenly, Christine heatedly complains that such language is not appropriate. Heather, who has the most salacious tongue, rolls her eyes and says, "Oh, Jesus, Christine." Christine turns to Ms. Philippoussis and says, "You need to do something about this." Heather turns up her palms and mutters something unintelligible.

Ms. Philippoussis answers, "The problem that concerns me is the ill feelings that are apparent between the two of you. We have lots of work to do and we need to cooperate, not fight among ourselves. Heather and Christine, is there a way we can settle this so you will both feel all right? Do you have any suggestions?"

Heather says, "Well, I don't like being singled out as the bad guy here."

"No," Ms. Philippoussis says, "the question is not who's right and wrong. Let's not even mention that. Let's just find a solution."

Both girls sit tight-lipped. Ms. Philippoussis then asks, "Christine, could you say in a respectful manner what you would like Heather to do differently?"

"Not cuss. That's offensive. We can do better than that. This is important work."

Ms. Philippoussis asks Heather what she would like Christine to do differently. Heather says, "I didn't hurt anybody. Can't we speak naturally without always having to think twice about what we say?"

Ms. Philippoussis persists, "And what would you like for Christine to do differently?"

"Not get hot under the collar. I don't feel I'm doing anything wrong."

Ms. Philippoussis says, "Perhaps we can't resolve this now. Let's call a truce for the rest of today's session. Before we meet next time, I hope the two of you will find a way to work things out. I'd like you to try. If you are unable to do so, we can ask the entire committee to discuss this matter and come to a fair agreement."

It may happen that before the next meeting, one or both of the girls will go to Ms. Philippoussis and tell her they have spoken and worked out their difficulty. That is what Ms. Philippoussis expects. But nothing is certain. She knows it is possible the girls won't iron out the problem and she will have to take further action. If that turns out to be the case, it would be well to have the committee discuss the situation, make a recommendation, and ask the girls to abide by it.

Scenario #4b. Stan and Belinda

In your English class, a boy named Stan sits directly behind a girl named Belinda. One day while students are reading at their seats, Belinda turns abruptly to face Stan and says loudly, "I said shut up! Are you sick or something?" This gets everyone's attention and brings classwork to a halt. You ask what is going on. Belinda and Stan look down and don't answer. Boys on each side of Stan have smiles on their faces.

All you know about the situation is what Belinda has done. Neither Belinda nor Stan seems willing to discuss the matter. Based on the information you have, what do you do? Try to answer this question before you read the next paragraph.

(What you have not been aware of) On each side of Stan sit two of his pals who laugh at everything he does. Stan rather likes Belinda and wants her to return his interest but doesn't know how to approach her properly. The class has been reading some of Chaucer's tales in modern English. In one of them the word "tit" is used. Stan whispers to Belinda loudly enough for his pals to hear, "Belinda, what does that word 'tit' mean?" His pals snicker. From that point on, Stan takes every opportunity to make barely-audible comments with sexual overtones. Belinda doesn't like it, but is uncomfortable about confronting him. She whispers from the side of her mouth, "Stop it!" Stan thinks she is playing along with him and that spurs him on. After three sessions Belinda is so sick of Stan's comments she finally turns around and says firmly, "I said shut up! Are you sick or something?"

If you were able to know what had been going on, you would have a better idea about how to proceed. What do you do if you are unable to get this information? If you do get the information, how might you proceed?

WHERE DO WE GO FROM HERE?

Please think through the items presented in the next section "To Think About." There you will find extensions of the discussions concerning the scenarios and other discipline matters. When you have done that, we will have completed our consideration of discipline in the synergetic classroom. You have seen that synergetic teaching eliminates most discipline problems but a few still arise now and then. Students may be able to resolve some of the matters themselves. When they can't, you need to help them. There is no set procedure to apply. What you do depends on your appraisal of the situation, your ability to identify the cause, and what you feel is best for the students involved.

In the next and final chapter we will consider how you can introduce synergetic teaching and discipline in your classes.

TO THINK ABOUT

When synergetic teaching is done as suggested, you will almost never have a student speak to you in a hostile or disrespectful manner. But we can't always get everything right. At times we may do or say something that offends a student and provokes a hostile response. At other times we may not be able to get enough information to act on. Little has been said about how we might respond helpfully when we can't get information or when students respond disrespectfully. Let's revisit two of the scenarios presented earlier and examine how the teachers might proceed under those circumstances.

1. Suppose in scenario #1b (Mrs. Nguyen suspects Ella of plagiarism) Mrs. Nguyen speaks with Ella about the paper. Ella takes immediate offense and exclaims, "You are saying I cheated! Well, I didn't! I'm not a cheat!" How should Mrs. Nguyen respond? Consider this possibility:

   • Ella, your paper is really beautifully presented. You have obviously put a lot of effort into it. I think, though, you might have misunderstood one thing about the assignment. I wanted you to put the ideas into your own words. Do you think you might do that? If you can, you will have a paper we can both feel good about. I'll help you with an example and then you can do the rest. (If Mrs. Nguyen had said this when she first approached Ella about the problem, everything would have remained calm.)

2. Think back to scenario #4b involving Stan and Belinda (sexual innuendos). As the teacher you want to settle altercations quickly, but equitably. Unless Stan and Belinda give you some information there is little you can do to help. You want to be careful about rushing to conclusions concerning what happened and who's at fault. If the students don't give you the information you need, what do you say to them? Consider these options:

   • Belinda and Stan, I'd like to help, but I don't understand what has upset you. I'm wondering if the two of you can settle the matter between you. Would you give it a try? Perhaps you will let me know tomorrow whether you've been able to do so.

   • Belinda, I see you are upset. I'd like to help resolve this matter, but I don't understand what caused it. Would the two of you, Stan and Belinda, meet with me for just a moment after class?

3. Regarding causes of misbehavior:

   • Do you feel the 10 causes shown in Figure 10.3 explain the origin of most misbehavior? Can you think of additional causes?

   • Many people believe that a major cause of misbehavior is students simply trying to see what they can get away with. Do you believe students misbehave for that reason? If so, can the gentle approach advocated in synergetic discipline help them?

4. The suggested strategies for resolving problems and conflicts focus on finding a solution that is acceptable to all involved. Suppose a student swears at you. What would you say to the student, in keeping with the synergetic philosophy of helpfulness?

11
GETTING STARTED IN SYNERGETIC TEACHING AND DISCIPLINE

Some thought Miss Simpson tried too hard to make a good first impression on her advanced chemistry students.

SUGGESTIONS FOR IMPLEMENTING SYNERGETIC TEACHING AND DISCIPLINE

Suppose you decide synergetic teaching and discipline would benefit you and your students. You have read the philosophy and mulled over the suggestions but are still unsure about how, exactly, to begin—what to do first, second, third, and so on. The following suggestions are presented for your consideration. They are not a prescribed regimen, so make adjustments as you see fit.

IDEALLY, SEVEN SESSIONS ARE NEEDED

It takes some time to install the synergetic approach because you must develop it in close collaboration with your students. The introduction is best made through a series of seven sessions. From third grade up, each of the sessions requires about 20 minutes or, in some cases, a bit more. For primary grades, the sessions can be completed in 10 to 15 minutes each. The following suggestions are generic in nature and aimed at sixth-or seventh-grade level. You can modify them to suit your schedule, students, and personal style. If you look back to Chapter 6 you can reread approaches taken by real teachers at grades kindergarten, three, six, and ten.

Sit in a Circle

For all of these sessions the students should be seated in a tight circle, if possible. If your classroom, lab, hall, or gymnasium doesn't provide flexible seating, make the best arrangement you can for students to have eye contact with each other. Explain that you will often want students to discuss matters and help make decisions about the class. Explain that such sessions are called class meetings and that the circular seating allows students to talk directly to each other, which helps them exchange ideas better.

Session #1. Opening Yourself to Students, and Students to You

Smile at the students as they come into the room. Look at their faces. Make eye contact. Say hello. When you have shown them how to get settled in a circle, tell them you are pleased to see them and are looking forward to working with them and that you have been thinking about some exciting possibilities for the class that you want to discuss with them. From the class list, call each student by name. Make eye contact and smile. Ask if you have pronounced the name correctly. Do your best to learn all names as quickly as possible—this is very important to students.

In language appropriate to their level, tell students a bit about yourself. Let your personality show. Describe your family if you have one. Mention any pets and tell what they are like. Also mention hobbies and special interests. Don't go into detail for the present, but as the class progresses add mention of traveling you have done, special skills you possess, unusual experiences you've had, and other items of interest. You might want to tell why you became a teacher and what you have liked most about it. Through anecdotes, tell something about your point of view regarding the following:

- Education—its value and what it can give people who take advantage of it

- Students—how you consider them all valuable and capable of learning and how the best part of teaching is doing all you can to help them
- Teaching—your views on how teachers best help students learn, by getting them interested rather than bossing or scolding them
- Life in general—the enormous privilege of being alive, the great adventures life brings, the challenges it poses, and the opportunities it gives us to make something good of ourselves

About halfway through the session, tell the students you'd like to learn something about them. From your class roster call on individual students. Ask if they have pets or brothers or sisters and what they are like. Call on as many students as time allows. As the session ends, thank them and tell them at the next session you would like to learn some of their feelings about school.

Session #2. Drawing Students out Regarding How They'd Like the Class to Function

Bring a chart and marker with you to the circle so you can take notes. Tell the students you are interested in conducting the class in a way that helps them learn important things and have an enjoyable time doing so. Begin by asking:

1. What are some of the things you like best about school?
   (They will probably say they like sports, being with friends, playing, and doing art and music. Some may mention performing in plays, concerts, and athletics. A few may mention learning, good teachers, computers, laboratories, and library.) Down the left side of your chart make a list of what they say.
2. Ask what they like, specifically, about each of the things you've written on the list. Write their comments on the right side of your chart.
3. Ask if they think any of the things they've mentioned might be possible in this class. Circle the things they feel would be possible.

Thank the students for their contributions. Tell them you want the class to include things they like, insofar as possible. Tell them you will consider their suggestions carefully and will make sure to use as many as you can.

Session #3. Feedback on Suggestions and Drawing Students out Concerning What They Prefer in Teachers

Before this session, redo the chart of suggestions made previously and indicate which of them you might be able to build into the class. Ask if they have other thoughts or suggestions. Turn to a fresh page on the chart. Elicit students' thoughts concerning the kind of teachers they prefer:

1. Ask if they have had a teacher they really enjoyed and respect-ed. Ask them not to mention names, but to indicate what that teacher did that made such a good impression. (They will prob-ably say the teacher was nice, interesting, helpful, fair, and had a sense of humor. They may mention activities they liked or special talents the teacher had.) Write the traits students men-tion down the left side of your chart.
2. Review the traits. Where needed, ask for elaboration, such as, What does a "nice" teacher do? What does a "helpful" teacher do? What does "we really had fun" mean? Make notes on the right side of the chart.
3. Tell students you hope to be the kind of teacher they prefer, insofar as you are able. Tell them you want time to study the notes you have made and will give them feedback at the next session. Thank them for their thoughtfulness.

Session #4. Feedback on Teacher Traits and Drawing Students out on Class Behavior

Before this session, make a clean copy of students' comments about traits they like in teachers. Begin the session by showing them the copy. Tell them this is what you understood them to say they liked in teach-ers. Ask if they have corrections or further suggestions. Tell them you will do your best to be the kind of teacher they say they like. (If they have made suggestions you can't comply with, tell them why.) Now draw students out regarding how they like their classmates to behave in school:

1. Ask students to think of a classmate who has behaved in ways they admired or appreciated. Without naming names, let them tell what the classmate was like. List the traits they mention down the left side of your chart.
2. When several behaviors are listed, go back and ask *why* those behaviors are appreciated. List the comments on the right side of the chart.
3. Move further by asking students how they like fellow members of classes to treat them. Make notes on the left side and go back and again ask *why*.
4. Now ask what kind of behavior they most appreciate from other students when they are working together on assignments. Ask why. Just before the end of the session ask the students if they all agree on the behaviors and reasons you have listed on your chart. When that question is settled, ask if they think it would be possible to have the kinds of behavior in this class-room that are listed on the chart.

Thank them for their input. Tell them that by the next session you will have their ideas written on a chart for review.

Session #5. Feedback on Desired Behavior and Exploration of Undesirable Behavior

Before this session, prepare a clean chart that shows the behaviors students said they most liked in their classmates.

1. Show students the chart of traits and reasons. Ask them if you have correctly understood their comments. Ask if any changes need to be made.

2. Now ask for their input concerning the kind of behavior they *dislike* in their classmates. On the left side of the chart make a list of the disliked behaviors. Ask students why they dislike them. Make notes concerning the reasons on the right side of the page.

3. When that is done, ask if they have ideas about how to keep those unwanted behaviors from occurring. Tell them you are interested in how to prevent the behaviors, not correct them after they have occurred. They may have some trouble with this. If they do, ask them if they are able to decide how they will behave, or if they have no control over what they do. They will probably agree they can control their behavior.

4. Ask what makes them decide to behave either properly or improperly. Ask students if there is anything you the teacher can do to help them *want* to behave properly. Take notes. If they get stuck, ask directly about the Golden Rule, making friends, caring about others, and having interesting things to do.

5. Once they have identified how you might help them want to behave properly, review their suggestions, then:

6. Say the following: Suppose despite everything we do, someone in the class decides to misbehave, to do something that we as a class do not approve of. What should we do then? How should we deal with that person? Students typically suggest punishment of some sort. If they do,

7. Say: I would want to help that person understand that this behavior is hurtful to the class. I wouldn't want to punish him. I don't want to be unpleasant or fight against any of you because that doesn't do either of us any good. What I would like to do, if possible, is fix whatever is causing the person to misbehave. That is how I would like to deal with misbehavior. What do you think of that? Put yourself in that student's place. Would you prefer being punished or having conditions changed so you wouldn't feel like misbehaving anymore?

Thank the students for taking this matter seriously. Tell them you will think about their suggestions and see if you can put together a plan for good class behavior to consider at the next meeting.

Session #6. Have Students Respond to Your Plan for Good Behavior in the Class

Before the session prepare a chart that shows the following: (1) Things students have said they like best in school, (2) Traits students have said they like best in teachers, (3) Behaviors students have said they like in classmates, (4) Behaviors students say they dislike in classmates, and (5) How you hope to help students want to behave properly.

1. Review the first four items on the chart. Ask if you have written what the students meant to say. When that is settled:

2. Review your plan for dealing with misbehavior, including:

   a) Why you believe students will have little reason to misbehave if school is interesting, students treat each other well, and the teacher is nice and helpful.
   b) How students can resolve most of their disputes in a friendly manner.
   c) How you will talk with students who misbehave to try to correct whatever is causing their misbehavior.

Ask the class to comment on the plan and make suggestions. End the session by thanking them and saying that at the next session you hope the class can formulate some agreements about what teacher and students can do to make the class enjoyable and worthwhile.

Session #7. Formulate the Class Agreements

Bring back the chart used in the previous session. Put it to the side but in view. Using a blank chart, tell the students you now hope they can finalize agreements that will guide the class. Ask students to help compose a succinct statement about each of the following:

1. Class activities that are valuable and enjoyable.
2. The teacher's way of teaching and treating students.
3. The students' ways of treating each other and the teacher.
4. How students will work at assigned tasks.

When satisfactory statements have been made, tell the class that you feel sure you can do what they have said concerning class activities and the way they like to be taught and treated. Ask individual students if they feel they could always follow the agreements they have made. Ask the group as a whole if anyone thinks they might not be able to do what the agreement says. When that is done, tell the class you will print out the agreements and display them in the room.

THE FOLLOWING DAYS AND WEEKS

You have already begun, through ethical and charismatic behavior, to attract students to you and build their trust. As you begin to know your students, you may find that one or more behave so distastefully you can hardly stand them. Yet you have determined you will do the best you can for each and every one of them. How do you overcome the great antipathy you feel?

Give this suggestion a good go: Try to find something positive or something attractive about the student. Anything. Begin focusing on that quality. Comment on it. Use it as an opening to get communication started between the two of you. Expand from that beginning to try to identify other qualities. The student may continue his unattractive behavior. Talk with him about it, but keep trying to expand the areas of quality you are discovering. Your personal attention and appreciation for the qualities will gradually make inroads. The kid's unattractive behavior will slowly change. Don't expect to make a silk purse of him, but do show appreciation for improvements. There is a good chance that over time you will have success with that student.

Meanwhile, with class agreements in place, you can occasionally bring up for discussion questions such as:

1. When you watch television do you ever see characters in the programs speak to each other in ways we don't approve of in our classroom? Can you think of any examples? Do you think the way they speak helps build good relationships between them? Do you think they have good ways of settling their problems? Why do you suppose television and movies show people having so much conflict? Why do you suppose they don't resolve their problems as we do in this class?

2. Have you seen any television programs or movies in the past few days that show people doing violence to each other? Why do you suppose so much violence is shown? Is that sort of violence something you would, in real life, like to be involved in? Is the violence in those programs and films being used to try to settle disagreements? Do you think violence is a good way for people to settle disputes? Can you suggest how they might do it better?

3. Do you think violence in television and movies is a good thing to show people? Do you think it teaches friendliness and respect for others? Do you ever see children imitating violent things characters do to each other? Do you think there is any chance children might believe, from what they see, that hostility and violence are the best ways to work out problems between people?

4. Outside of our classroom, say on the grounds or in the cafeteria, do you ever hear students get angry with each other? So angry they call each other names and feel like fighting? In our class we try hard to settle disputes by having the people involved talk together calmly and respectfully until they find a solution that suits everyone. Do you feel you can use that

process outside the class as well, if you get involved in a dispute? What do you think the other person would do if you remained calm and asked if the two of you could talk the matter over respectfully?

In addition to holding discussions such as these in conjunction with teaching students how to resolve problems and conflicts, you proceed systematically installing and strengthening the other elements that contribute to synergy—good communication, interesting learning topics and activities, coopetition where appropriate, and good human relations skills. Discuss with students all the things you are doing to make the class a better place for them and continue modeling the behaviors you would like students to emulate.

QUESTIONS AND ANSWERS ABOUT SYNERGETIC TEACHING AND DISCIPLINE

1. Synergetic teaching seems to be a panacea. Can it really be as good as all that?
   Answer: If by panacea you mean an approach that corrects all problems and invariably works as envisioned, the answer is no. Synergetic teaching and discipline give results that are very good indeed, but not perfect. However, if you conscientiously apply the synergetic approach as suggested, you will see improvements all around in teaching, discipline, and student attitude.

2. If the synergetic approach is capable of producing such good results, why hasn't it been discovered before?
   Answer: It has been, in a way. Some very successful teachers have used it for a long time. They never thought of it as a way of producing synergy. They simply had a natural knack for working with the young in a helpful, respectful manner. The results proved to be good for everyone.

3. How much time has to be given to class meetings? As a mathematics teacher I can't spend time on discussing other matters. I can barely get the material covered as it is.
   Answer: The seven initial sessions take about two-and-a-half hours. For your class a weekly 20-minute class meeting should be held to deal with class concerns. The meetings and discussions do require time, but you will recoup it all, and more, by not having to deal with discipline so much. In addition, students will be more cooperative, have a better attitude, work harder, and treat you better.

4. The facilitative teaching approach that is advocated in synergetic teaching has been tried before and more or less abandoned

as ineffective. Why advocate a teaching method that has not been popular with teachers?

Answer: Consider the difference between directive and facilitative teaching. In directive teaching, the teacher does everything—selects topics, plans lessons, organizes activities, selects instructional materials, gives instructional input such as lecture or demonstration, observes students while they practice the new skill or information, corrects errors, and later evaluates how well they have done. This is the method most teachers now use, though they put their personal touches on it. It gained strong favor in the early 1980s as an efficient way to teach factual information and certain skills, but it is clearly ineffective in helping students develop reasoning, judgment, and self-discipline. Moreover, it rests on the presumptions that students will be interested in what they are being taught, will enjoy the experience, and will behave themselves. Experience has shown that those presumptions do not stand up. Directive teaching therefore requires a discipline system strong enough to make students pay attention, stick to their work, and refrain from various misbehaviors even when they are not interested in the lesson or activities.

Facilitative teaching does not call for detailed plans in advance. It leaves considerable leeway. In order to work well, it requires the trust and good will of the students. Also, the students must feel they have helped decide on the working arrangements in the class, which they do through individual and group decisions and agreements. When you allow students more than token input into making decisions about learning and behavior, you can't at the same time use a directive teaching approach in which you make all the decisions. In synergetic teaching, you work constantly to maintain trust, goodwill, and interest. You don't have to direct everything, nor worry about keeping a lid on misbehavior. When students become involved in activities they find interesting, you can function in a helping role, opening up possibilities, raising questions, making suggestions, helping locate resources, and encouraging students to do work they are proud of.

5. Am I right that synergetic teaching tries to make everything in the class fun and enjoyable? That is not realistic for life either in or out of school. Some of the things we need to learn are simply not fun, but that doesn't mean we disregard them.

Answer: The classroom needn't reflect the larger society. Rather, it should be a place of greater humanity and deeper concern for others than is the case outside school. Through education we want to help students become not only knowledgeable and skillful, but also self-directing, ethical, concerned about others, and able to resolve disputes amicably. They learn those behaviors through imitation and practice, and retain them if they see their value in wider life.

With regard to everything in class being always fun and enjoyable, obviously that cannot always be the case. But it can be most of the time. Students will engage willingly in activities they find enjoyable, satisfying, and useful. They resist activities they find boring or meaningless. That resistance brings on the misbehavior, lethargy, and poor attitude that we are trying so hard to correct. Those are facts of classroom life. We do students and ourselves a big favor when we find ways to make learning as enjoyable as possible.

If your curriculum includes topics that are inherently dull, perhaps ones that former students have disliked, test them against these two questions:

a) Is this something my students really *need* to know in order to lead better lives?

b) Will my students encounter this topic on achievement or college-entrance exams?

If the answer to both questions is no, drop the topic even if it is listed in the curriculum guide and featured in the textbook. If the answer to either question is yes, then teach the topic, but deliver it through activities students are known to enjoy, such as challenge, mystery, role-playing, or working together. Explain to the students why you consider the topic essential. Ask for their cooperation.

6. By letting students make so many decisions about what to learn and how to behave, aren't we putting the inmates in charge of the asylum? Don't we know better than students what they need to learn and how they should conduct themselves? We teachers are supposed to be the experts, aren't we?

   Answer: Experts yes. And because of our understanding about human nature, we realize we can reach our goals only when students willingly behave and involve themselves in learning. We know that trying to force their compliance is worse than futile, so we do what we can to make learning appealing.

7. Is it realistic to believe that all students will happily comply with class agreements, even when they have helped compose them and promised to abide by them? Even in the best classes students often daydream, act out, or do less than their best work. Why have them agree to something they can't live up to?

   Answer: The agreements are similar to laws in the sense that they show what we collectively believe to be the best and fairest way to function. Laws get broken and so do class agreements. But the process of involving students in formalizing the agreements causes them to feel they can, and should, abide by them. They are much more likely to comply with agreements they have helped establish than with commandments we hand down to them. The agreements themselves should be clear and we should expect students to abide by them. We wouldn't make a law that sets the speed limit at 70, give or take whatever your mood suggests at a given time. Nor would we agree in class to treat others as we would like to be treated, except when we are upset or in a bad mood. We should expect the agreements to be followed all the time. When they are not, we look first to ourselves to see if we are responsible for the daydreaming or failure to give best effort. If we satisfy ourselves we are not to blame, then we look for other causes.

8. How does synergetic teaching provide for students with special needs? My classes usually enroll two or three such students, commonly with attention deficit disorder. Those students can't pay attention or stick to their work for long and they cause lots of trouble.

   Answer: Your initial approach is to deal with them just like you do other students, though you may work harder to develop a trusting relationship through kindness, encouragement, help, and personal talks. As they come to trust and like you, they will show more consideration but will not be perfect. Given the sense of family you are developing in the class, other students will understand the difficulty and help the student or disregard misbehavior when it occurs. If the children have been identified as having special needs, you will probably also receive some expert help.

9. Synergetic teaching seems to require so much extra work and effort, do you think teachers will seriously consider using it? They are already tired and don't need extra work to do.

   Answer: Synergetic teaching doesn't add to the teacher's workload. Once it gets underway, it is just as easy as typical teaching and immeasurably more satisfying. Most of the elements that lead to synergy have to do with teacher behavior, in particular communication and ways of relating to students. Those approaches don't require more time or work. It does take some time to reach good class agreements, but not much effort is required. It may take a little time to begin adding interest to dull lessons and to organize coopetition, but the extra work is relatively inconsequential. The payoff, on the other hand, is large. Instead of feeling more tired and put-upon, teachers will feel more satisfied and content.

10. Don't you feel that synergetic teaching and discipline put all the onus on teachers? They have to make all the accommodations to suit students. Students don't do anything. Where is their responsibility in the equation?

    Answer: It is true that the onus falls on the teacher, but the burden is not heavy. Yes, synergetic teachers do make accommodations to student needs, interests, and preferences, while students don't have to put anything into the process. But that is the price we pay in order to teach today's kids successfully. If we wait for students to make an accommodation to what pleases us, we'll have a long wait. Perhaps it seems demeaning for teachers to do all the adjusting, but professionally it is the correct thing to do. It provides great benefits for students and, in return, for teachers.

11. Great claims are made for synergetic teaching and discipline. Are there any studies that support these claims?

    Answer: No, there have been no studies conducted to test synergetic teaching per se—the synergetic approach has not previously been set forth formally. But its elements and suggestions come from the teachings of renowned psychologists, psychiatrists, counselors, and, perhaps most tellingly, from the experiences of outstanding teachers. Moreover, synergetic teaching makes logical sense in terms of what we know about human nature and behavior.

12. In my school we have a schoolwide discipline plan that is working well. Would there be any advantage in replacing it with synergetic discipline?

    Answer: Synergetic discipline is part and parcel of synergetic teaching. It can't be separated so as to stand on its own irrespective of how teaching is done. In any case, if you and the students are well satisfied with the discipline program now in place, there is no reason to change.

REMINDER CARDS

As you begin putting synergetic teaching and discipline in place, there are a number of things you need to remember. For your convenience, the following reminder cards are presented. They include hints and suggestions that, when practiced, will help bring the nine elements of synergy to full functioning. For convenience you might wish to photocopy the reminder cards and laminate them. You can use them to remind yourself of skills to work on and also for self-analysis and evaluation. Try to practice selected skills every day. Through diligent practice you will make them part of your natural behavior.

Ethics and Trust

- Your ETHICAL BEHAVIOR builds STUDENT TRUST, which is needed for SYNERGY.
- Ethical behavior means always doing the right thing when dealing with students.
- Seven ethical principles you must demonstrate to students through your behavior are:

  1. **Kindness**. Treat each and every student with kindness, always.

  2. **Consideration**. Always allow troubled students to maintain their self-respect.

  3. **Faith**. Make evident your sincere belief in the potential of every student.

  4. **Helpfulness**. Try to do, in any circumstance, what would be most helpful to students.

  5. **Fairness**. Show no favoritism. Treat all students justly.

  6. **Honesty**. Always be honest with students, but use tact to protect their dignity.

  7. **Patience**. Be tolerant of mistakes. Keep trying. Don't give up on students.

Charisma

- CHARISMA is the overall quality of your personality that attracts students to you.
- Students of charismatic teachers are more cooperative and less prone to misbehavior.
- Charismatic teachers bring positive excitement and often produce synergy in their classes.
- These traits are usually evident in charismatic teachers–make them part of your behavior:

    1. **Smiles** and **positive body carriage**. Smile frequently. Stand and walk confidently.

    2. **Friendliness**. Use students' names, chat with them, show you are glad they are there.

    3. **Enthusiasm**. Act happily upbeat about students, school activities, and life in general.

    4. **Sensitivity**. Pick up on students' feelings. Take them into account as you teach.

    5. **Compassion**. Show consideration and understanding when students feel troubled.

- Here are ways to increase your charisma. Try them and see how they work.

    1. **Chat purposefully with students**. Open them up, learn about them, remember it.
    2. **Tell something about your personal life**. Family, pets, interests, hobbies, travels.
    3. **Relate notable experiences**. Not too often, not too much. Just enough to pique interest.
    4. **Share special skills**. If you are really good at something, let kids know. Show them.
    5. **Share special knowledge**. Tell students about unusual things you have learned.
    6. **Present yourself memorably**. Do positive things that help set you apart from others.
    7. **Show unconditional professional love for students**. Be forever accepting and helpful.

Communication

- Good communication is crucial in setting the stage for class synergy.
- Communication at its best involves *exchanging* information, back and forth, with students.
- Things you the teacher must strive to do to make communication go well:

  1. **Listen before you talk**. Show receptiveness. Encourage students to talk. Listen to them.

  2. **Understand the student's message**. Try to see things from the student's point of view.

  3. **Respond helpfully**. Be encouraging. Never attack students or put them down.

  4. **Never argue with students**. You cannot win. Arguing only produces negative results.

- Set up structures that facilitate and enhance communication. Consider the following:

  1. Systematically give students **informal personal attention**. Chat as often as possible.

  2. Schedule sessions to **review students' feelings** about the class and activities.

  3. Hold regular **class meetings** where students discuss and resolve class problems.

  4. Schedule times for **speaking privately** with students whether or not there are problems.

  5. **Inform parents** about class activities and how their child is progressing.

Making School Interesting

- Students are becoming disenchanted with school, complaining it is boring and irrelevant.
- By presenting interesting topics and activities, we can make school appealing to students.
- For subjects and topics that are naturally dull, we can add activities that students enjoy.

continued

Making School Interesting (cont.)

- If you expect students to behave well you must meet their psychological needs, which are:

    1. **Security**. They must feel safe from physical and psychological danger.

    2. **Hope**. They must feel they can succeed in and gain valuable benefits from school.

    3. **Acceptance**. They must feel they are important to the teacher and the class.

    4. **Dignity**. Their sense of self must remain whole. It must not be attacked or denigrated.

    5. **Power**. They must feel they have some say in making class decisions that affect them.

    6. **Enjoyment**. They must experience fun and satisfaction in class activities.

    7. **Competence**. They must feel they are acquiring skills and knowledge important in life.

- You can help students take renewed interest and behave better by doing the following:

    1. **Get to know your students**–what they are like, interested in, and predisposed to do.

    2. **Adapt instruction** to make it consonant with student nature and meet students' needs.

    3. **Give students choice** in helping select topics of interest and ways they prefer to learn.

    4. **Spice up** topics that are naturally dull with activities students enjoy.

    5. **Use facilitative rather than directive teaching**. Lead the students, don't boss them.

- If you have to teach dull topics, overlay them with one or more of the following:

physical movement	novelty	mystery	adventure	drama
story telling	challenge	excursions	guests	role playing
rhythmic activities	acting out	music	cooperation	competition

- Remember, students usually do **not** like the following:

sitting still for long periods	keeping quiet for long periods	working alone
memorizing facts for tests	lengthy written assignments	busy work

Class Agreements

- Class agreements establish the **kind of behavior and instruction** to prevail in the class.
- Class agreements should mention **teaching style, learning activities, and class behavior**.
- Class agreements reflect the **full consideration and consent** of both students and teacher.
- Class agreements indicate what **is expected** and are referred to when transgressed.
- One way to help students formulate agreements is to follow these steps:

  1. Ask students what they **enjoy most about school**. Take notes on a chart or chalkboard.

  2. Ask students what they **dislike most about school**. Continue taking notes.

  3. Ask students what they like have **liked in their favorite teachers**.

  4. Ask students what they have **disliked most in their teachers**.

  5. Ask students how they **prefer to work** in class–what kinds of activities they enjoy.

  6. Ask students which class **activities they dislike** most.

  7. Ask students to identify topics or subjects they don't enjoy but believe necessary to learn.

  8. Ask students how they like **classmates to treat them**, and what they don't like.

  9. Collate and list what they **enjoy and prefer**. These are emphasized in class agreements.

  10. Collate and list what they **dislike**. The agreement may indicate these are to be avoided.

  11. Make a chart that lists "what we like" and "what we dislike." Then help students:

  12. Compose succinct statements that describe teacher and student behavior in the class.

What We Like	*What We Dislike*
(list)	(list)

Our Class Agreements
(a few concise statments)

Coopetition

- "Coopetition" **combines cooperation and competition**; it includes the best of both.

- Coopetition is a process in which students **cooperate in order to compete**.

- Coopetition is ineffective for very young children but **powerful for those past age eight.**

- Coopetition combines the strengths of *cooperation* (enjoyment, divergence of ideas, distribution of work load, better overall product, and learning to work together) with the strengths of *competition* (self-direction, independent thinking, responsibility, and efficiency). At the same time it eliminates the weaknesses of cooperation (uneven work burden, lack of personal responsibility, and lack of initiative) and of competition (sense of isolation, demoralization from never winning, and inclination to defend one's performance by lying and cheating).

- In Coopetition, students work cooperatively in groups to compete against other groups.

- Coopetition is especially useful in the following situations:
  1. Group work trying to surpass pre-set standards or previous group records.
  2. Competition among groups in the class.
  3. Competition against other classes or schools.
  4. Attempting to exceed expectations.

- Coopetition is **not appropriate** in lessons that involve experiencing (e.g. observing, touching, listening, describing) rather than high achievement in skills and knowledge.

Human Relations

- Human relations concerns **how we treat people and get along with them**.
- Teachers should **model the best human relations** and teach those skills to their students:
  1. Smiling and greeting others pleasantly.
  2. Using positive body language, such as eye contact and gestures that indicate acceptance.
  3. Sending clear verbal messages to others.
  4. Being mindful of how our words sound (e.g., calm, forceful, demanding, sarcastic).
  5. Reacting positively to what others say and do.
  6. Following through on agreements.
  7. Conferring dignity on others.

- **Conferring dignity** on others is highly important and is accomplished as follows:
  1. Paying **genuine attention** to others.
  2. Asking their **opinion**.
  3. Listening to them empathetically, trying to understand **within their frame of reference**.
  4. **Following up** on what they say by mentioning it or acting on it.
  5. Drawing **public attention** to their contributions.

- What we must avoid when trying for good human relations:
  1. Showing **lack of interest** in the other person.
  2. **Slighting** the other person.
  3. **Putting down** the other person.
  4. **Speaking sarcastically** to, or about, the other person.

Gentle Discipline in the Synergetic Classroom

- Discipline problems are situations where students **notably transgress** class agreements.
- When your class begins to function **synergetically,** few discipline problems will occur.

  You will reach that point when you do the following:
  1. Established fair and reasonable class agreements that students **agree with and buy into.**
  2. Developed a sense of family in the class, where **students help and look out for each other.**

continued

Gentle Discipline in the Synergetic Classroom (cont.)

　　3. Put into practice the **nine elements of synergetic teaching:** ethics, trust, charisma, communication, interest, class agreements, coopetition, human relations, and problem resolution.

- When discipline problems occur, deal with them in a **helpful, nonconfrontive manner.** Never attack students verbally. Don't argue. Don't put them down. Don't back them into a corner. Show continual willingness to help resolve what is bothering them.

- In synergetic discipline, you **first** direct attention to the **cause of misbehavior.** Take your time there. Make sure you have the facts straight so you identify the correct cause, which might be:

　　1. Probing boundaries
　　2. Mimicking others
　　3. Strong curiosity or interest in something
　　4. Desire for attention
　　5. Desire for power
　　6. Boredom or frustration
　　7. Emotionality from something that happened outside class
　　8. Threat to dignity
　　9. Disagreements that escalate and boil over
　　10. Egocentric personality

- (Occasionally students misbehave because they have psychological or medical difficulties. These cases require expert help which your school system will provide.)

- Second, you correct the cause by eliminating or modifying it. When in doubt about the cause, ask students about the behavior. Ask if there is a problem you can help with or ask, "Can you help me understand why this is happening? I'd like to help fix the problem." Show you are not interested in punishing but only in correcting the cause. For the egocentric personality, this takes some time but can be accomplished through trust and helpfulness.

- Third, should a conflict arise between you and the student, remain calm. Drop your defenses. Donít struggle against the student. Be positive and helpful. Your challenge is to win the student over. The more often you do that, the more students will trust you and cooperate.

- Finally, donít take misbehavior personally. When you teach synergetically, you are interacting with students in a professional, caring manner. If students misbehave, itís not your fault. You are not the cause. Rest assured in that knowledge and continue doing your best to help.

Resolving Nondisciplinary Problems and Conflicts

- Nondisciplinary means **no misbehavior** is involved, no breach of class agreements.
- Problems are situations that affect the class **seriously enough** to require attention.
- If no personal conflict is involved, the following steps are used to resolve class problems:

    1. In class discussion, **clarify the problem**. Try to state exactly what is occurring and why.

    2. **Identify possible solutions**. Use brainstorming. List ideas on the board or a chart.

    3. From the suggestions, **select one or more** that are likely to produce the desired results.

    4. **Try out** the proposed solution. See how it works in practice. Modify it if necessary.

- Conflicts are **emotional disputes** between two or more people and often involve the teacher. They are best resolved through the *win/win process*, conducted as follows:

    1. Each disputant **explains their concern** and why they are troubled.

    2. Each disputant listens to the other and tries genuinely to **see their point of view**.

    3. Disputants try to identify possible solutions that would be **fully acceptable to both**.

    4. Disputants select and **implement a solution**, if possible. They may need arbitration.

- When teachers have conflicts with students, they should **control themselves** as follows:

    1. Focus on the **behavior**, not the student.

    2. Deal with the **present moment**; don't bring up past history.

    3. Take charge of negative emotions. **Remain calm and objective**.

    4. Allow students to **save face.** Don't back them into a corner.

REFERENCES

Albert, L. 1996. *Cooperative discipline*. Circle Pines, MN: American Guidance Service.

Biddulph, S. 1997. *Raising boys*. Sydney, Australia: Finch Publishing.

Canter, L. 1976. *Assertive discipline: A take-charge approach for today's educator*. Seal Beach, CA: Canter & Associates.

Canter, L. and M. Canter. 1993. *Succeeding with difficult students; New strategies for reaching your most challenging students*. Santa Monica, CA: Canter & Associates.

Carnegie, D. 1981. *How to win friends and influence people*. Revised edition. New York: Pocket Books.

Charles, C. 1974. *Teachers' Petit Piaget*. Belmont, CA: Fearon.

Collis, J. 1998. *When your customer wins, you can't lose*. Sydney, Australia: HarperBusiness.

Coloroso, B. 1994. *Kids are worth it! Giving your child the gift of inner discipline*. New York: William Morrow.

Covey, S. 1989. *The seven habits of highly effective people*. New York: Simon & Schuster.

Curwin, R. 1992. *Rediscovering hope: Our greatest teaching strategy*. Bloomington, IN: National Educational Service.

Curwin, R. and A. Mendler. 1988. *Discipline with dignity*. Alexandria, VA: Association for Supervision and Curriculum Development.

Dreikurs, R. and P. Cassel. 1972. *Discipline without tears*. New York: Hawthorne.

Dreikurs, R., B. Grunwald, and F. Pepper. 1982. *Maintaining sanity in the classroom*. Reissued in 1998. New York: Taylor & Francis.

Ginott, H. 1971. *Teacher and child*. New York: Macmillan.

Glasser, W. 1969. *Schools without failure*. New York: Harper and Row.

———. 1986. *Control theory in the classroom*. New York: Harper and Row.

———. 1992. *The quality school: Managing students without coercion*. New York: Harper and Row.

———. 1993. *The quality school teacher*. New York: Harper Perennial.

Gordon, T. 1970. *Parent effectiveness training: A tested new way to raise responsible children*. New York: New American Library.

———. 1974. *T.E.T.: Teacher effectiveness training*. New York: David McKay.

———. 1976. *P. E. T. in action*. New York, Random House.

———. 1989. *Discipline that works: Promoting self-discipline in children*. New York: Random House.

Jones, F. 1987. *Positive classroom discipline*. New York: McGraw-Hill.

Kohn, A. 1996. *Beyond discipline: From compliance to community*. Alexandria, VA: Association for Supervision and Curriculum Development.

Kounin, J. 1971. *Discipline and group management in classrooms*. Revised edition,1977. New York: Holt, Rinehart & Winston.

Nelsen, J., L. Lott, and H. Glenn. 1997. *Positive discipline in the classroom*. Rocklin, CA: Prima.

Piaget, J. 1951. *Judgment and reasoning in the child*. London: Routledge & Kegan Paul.

Redl, F. and W. Wattenberg. 1959. *Mental hygiene in teaching*. Revised edition. New York: Harcourt, Brace & World. (Book originally published in 1951.)

Skinner, B. 1954. The science of learning and the art of teaching. *Harvard Educational Review,* 24, 86-97.

Slavin, R. 1991. Synthesis of research on cooperative learning. *Educational Leadership,* 48,71-82.

Spence, G. 1995. *How to argue and win every time*. New York: St. Martin's Press.

INDEX